END OF THE RAINBOW
AND END OF THE ROUTE
KEY WEST US 1 FLORIDA
Unlimited Opportunities
TROPICAL VACATIONLAND

MOUNT ROBSON PARK

10633283

RIVER RUN COOKBOOK

Old photo of River Run

RIVER RUN COOKBOOK

Southern Comfort from Vermont

by Jimmy and Maya Kennedy
and Marialisa Calta

FOREWORD BY DAVID MAMET
AFTERWORD BY HOWARD NORMAN

HarperCollins*Publishers*

FIRST EDITION

Library of Congress Cataloging-in-Publication Data
Kennedy, Jimmy.
River Run Cookbook: Southern Comfort from Vermont / by Jimmy and Maya
Kennedy and Marialisa Calta.
p. cm.
Includes index.
ISBN 0-06-019525-8
1. Cookery, American. 2. River Run (Restaurant)   I. Kennedy, Maya.   II. Calta,
Marialisa.   III. Title.
TX715.K3545   2001
641.5'09743'4—dc21
00-040751

01 02 03 04 05 BT 10 9 8 7 6 5 4 3 2 1

CONTENTS

ACKNOWLEDGMENTS

River Run is not only a restaurant but, as we hope these pages will show, a gathering place for friends and neighbors. So we must first thank our customers for their continued support and good will, and their hearty appetites.

We thank our staff—past and present—for their hard work, loyalty and good humor.

To our agent, Liv Blumer, and to our editor, Susan Friedland: Thank you both for seeing a book in a tiny, little-known restaurant in small-town Vermont.

To the folks at HarperCollins who worked so hard: Vanessa Stich, Lucy Albanese, Lisa Bullaro, Kate Stark, Tom Lau, Richard Klin, Virginia Kroft, Kate Nichols, and Cathy Dorsey.

A special thanks (in no particular order) to those of you who have, over the years, shared your recipes: Josh Grinker, Steve Bogart, Anna Woolf, Nessa Rabin, Nicole Graves, Marty Levin, Bryna Levin, Tiny Heard, Kenneth McGeehee, Rhea Wilson, Trevis Gleason, Benjamin Cevelo, Aunt Hazel Schissler, and Steve Owens.

To Rick Levy, town constable and house photographer, thanks for bringing River Run to life. To others who donated photos (Michael Belenky, David Mamet, Mary Murphy, Andrew Nemethy, Jim Percelay, and Dirk Van Susteren) thanks to you, as well. We wish we could have included pictures of all of our customers—if yours didn't get in, thanks for understanding.

We would like to give a special thanks to a few of our loyal customers and friends, Larry Mires among them. Beverly Bradley and Mary Etta Chase who along with their husbands, Frank and Melvin, and friends, have been early morning regulars ever since we opened. Also a big thank you to Conrad Dix and Dennis Blair who are always willing to lend a hand when Jimmy needs help fixing or installing things at the restaurant. Denise Wands and Gregg Bradley for everything they have done and continue to do for River Run. And to Lisa Lackey, our original partner at River Run, who helped us get started on the right foot. To Ian Anderson and Ed Cecchi, our new partners in the River Run sauce business, thank you for your energy and enthusiasm in promoting all things River Run.

Thanks to the writers who grace not only our tables, but also the pages of this book: David Mamet and Howard Norman. Gratitude too, to Amy B. Trubek and Carol Parmenter for their kind words. Kudos, always, to cartoonist Ed Koren.

Moms are important to this book: Ours contributed not only recipes, but a lifetime of teaching about food and family. So, deepest gratitude to our mothers: Carolyn Kennedy Bowen, Charlotte Potok, and Diana Calta. The others in our families helped immeasurably, tasting recipes and rooting for us. Marialisa thanks her aunt, Antoinette Calta, and her husband and daughters-Dirk, Hannah, and Emma Van Susteren. Jimmy and Maya thank their family and friends, including Jimmy's brothers, Joseph Scott Kennedy and John Philip Kennedy. Jimmy would also like to acknowledge his dad, the late Jimmy "Cotton" Kennedy, who would have enjoyed sharing in the food and the fun.

Lastly, the newest member of the River Run team deserves a special mention: Josephine James Kennedy, who, at two, counts among her favorite foods fried catfish and grits.

FOREWORD

**David Mamet and Family—
Rebecca Pidgeon, Clara and Noah**

Jules Rabin was my philosophy teacher back in the sixties. I was sitting, my head in my hands, one day when he came up the path. He laid a hand on my shoulder and said, "Don't worry, it all gets easier when you turn thirty."

He was off by about ten years, but nonetheless I am grateful to him for a most useful bit of philosophy.

In the seventies Jules decided to go straight. He and his wife, Helen, toured Europe learning to make bread. They returned to Plainfield, Vermont, the scene of the late teaching career, and built a medieval stone beehive oven and set out to make—and continue to make—the world's best bread.

Often, we tell each other up here, the myrmidons of Zabar's and other down-country forces fly up to plead with the

Rabins to bake for them, but no, the story goes, the Rabins have read *Faust* and they are happy where they are.

Plainfield is the oddest community. It lies athwart Route Two between Montpelier and St. Johnsbury, and, since the war it has attracted the finest people.

The community ethos is a mix of the much-lauded but nonetheless real Yankee ingenuity and a sort of G.I. Bill: "If I've got a book on the subject and enough time, I *will* figure it out." For the woods are full of the most improbably accomplished people—potters, blacksmiths, weavers, cooks, many writers.

I never could imagine what went on at those arts colonies of which one reads. My vision has it something like a terrarium with typing and a lot of serious folk too busy thinking about form to gossip about who's sleeping with whom.

Not so Plainfield.

The area, in the thirty-plus years I've lived here, remains one of magnificent woods, grown back from given-up farms, the farmhouses peopled, now and then, by the bitten.

I used to play poker at a farmhouse above Plainfield, up on East Hill.

Once, in the middle of the night, I accepted a St. Bernard puppy for a fifty-dollar bet. The puppy's name was Elizabeth; and I remember, as the game began to fold, the children of the house came down for breakfast and a little girl played with the dog which had been mine till someone hit the gut-straight.

That little girl, and thank you for waiting, grew into and in fact *is* Maya Kennedy, who with her husband, Jimmy, owns and runs River Run Restaurant, and whose cookbook you now hold in your hands.

Cookbooks, to me, are magic.

x

Once, in a flurry of children, my wife responded to the essential male question, "What's for dinner?" with the unusual and terrifying answer, "You know where the cookbooks are, you know the way to the store." Oh, Lord.

All unbelief and doubt, I hauled down a cookbook, transcribed the ingredients, went to the store, et cetera, et cetera, and was and am astonished that what emerged, after a time, was absolutely recognizable as dinner.

Now, perhaps it was a fluke, and perhaps my report is, in that most dismissive of scientific terms, "anecdotal evidence," but I followed the directions, and I got food.

Perhaps this accounts for the popularity of cookbooks.

(I always thought they existed to keep the bookends from unseemly contact.)

Let me, then, with the blessing, wrench the shying, rearing horses of my two disparate themes, Vermont and the cookbook, into the one yoke and try to get them to pull together.

Here you have your Vermont cookbook. This is the real thing.

This is the food you'd eat if you were lucky enough to be sitting in the River Run Restaurant.

There you might be waited upon by Nessa Rabin, Jules and Helen's daughter; you would drink excellent coffee out of mugs made up the hill by Charlotte Potok, Maya's mom; you would have Rabin bread with your eggs, and Jimmy's catfish for dinner.

You would overhear the clientele talk about bass fishing or turkey hunting or would hear the writers bitching about publishers, or the farmers and the truckers talking low in the corner.

It would be picturesque if it weren't perfect.

David Mamet

Old picture of River Run when it was
the Post Office

INTRODUCTION

A DAY AT RIVER RUN

Sometimes, when I come here, I just eat dinner for breakfast," says Town Constable Rick Levy. He is sitting at the tiny River Run counter, tucking into a plate of smothered pork chops, a handmade pottery mug filled with steaming coffee plunked at his side. In front of him, through a pass-through window, a narrow slice of the kitchen and its crew is visible: Jimmy's seemingly headless torso stretches and bends as he hefts cast-iron fry pans and heavy pots from one burner to another, to the counter and back. The strings on the back of the dishwasher's apron bob up and down as their owner works over the deep, stainless-steel sink. The phone rings: an arm holding the receiver emerges from the pass-through, and a disembodied voice calls a customer's name. Jimmy's wife, Maya, stands near the cash register, holding the couple's baby, Josie.

Jules Rabin, who—with his wife, Helen—opened one of the first artisanal bakeries in the area in the late seventies, comes in with brown paper sacks full of crusty sourdough French and chewy rye bread. He stops to chat with his daughter, Nessa, who is a waitress. A carpenter orders a veggie scrambler. "I'm low on fuel," he says. A house painter comes in to have his thermos filled. "This place is one-quarter of my social life," he says.

Here are some other people who are at the restaurant this day: Graciela Monteagudo, an Argentine-born puppeteer, and her young son, Jan. David Mamet, the playwright, and his wife, actress Rebecca Pidgeon. David Hathaway, a house painter and chef. A woman in a long skirt and Birkenstocks, who

xiii

orders bacon but asks Jimmy to burn it. "I'm a vegetarian," she says, by way of explanation. Charlotte Potok, Maya's mother, who makes the pottery mugs and plates that grace River Run tables. The novelist Howard Norman, his wife, poet Jane Shore, and their daughter Emma. Three men who cut brush for the local electric cooperative, one of them complaining of a hangover. Gary Graves, mechanic and high school soccer coach. A piano tuner. Several members of the volunteer fire department. Artist Roy Levin. Larry Mires, a customer so loyal he is known as the Ambassador of River Run. Three Goddard College students wearing their hair in Rasta braids. A man who says he is related to William Shakespeare (through a bastard son) and who orders take-out. Jim Higgins, a writer and teacher, who likes to point out the wear marks on the wood floor left by a former occupant, Bill the Barber. "He had Parkinson's," says Higgins. "But when he cut hair, his hand was steady as a rock." Sue Brown, the general manager of nearby Lylehaven Farm, known as "Lady Lylehaven" to her crew.

"You know what I like?" says Monteagudo, the puppeteer. "It's the way this place brings different kinds of people together. Truck drivers. Artists. Hippies. Farmers. That doesn't happen in most places."

Here are some of the things that people are eating: biscuits and sausage gravy, meat loaf omelets, Jo-Jos, pulled pork, fried catfish, Patrick's Fancy Homes, oatmeal, banana pancakes, gumbo, fried chicken salad with buttermilk dressing, toast, veggie scramblers, bacon, brownies, okra fritters. And coffee. Lots of coffee. In colorful handmade mugs.

A BRIEF HISTORY OF RIVER RUN

On the main street of Plainfield, Vermont (pop. 1,300), across from the white clapboard United Methodist Church and backed right up against the Winooski River, sits a tiny, lopsided building with a beckoning porch: River Run.

Built in 1900, the 1½-story Cape has served the town in several capacities, including post office, speakeasy, and barbershop. Inside, the wooden floorboards still show the wear patterns marking traffic around Bill the Barber's long-gone chair.

Maya (Clifford) Kennedy grew up in Plainfield; as a teenager, she used to hang out at the stone wall across the street from what is now River Run. Jimmy Kennedy was raised in Brewer, Mississippi, just outside Tupelo. The pair met in New York City in the eighties—Maya was working as a graphic artist, and Jimmy was selling catfish and was a partner in two restaurants, Nadine's and the Acme Bar & Grill. They returned to Maya's hometown and got married.

In 1991, Maya and Jimmy Kennedy opened River Run. Jimmy's in the kitchen; Maya runs the front of the house. The wear patterns on the wooden floors are getting deeper.

RIVER RUN TODAY

River Run is, first and foremost, a breakfast place. One just has to be imaginative in defining "breakfast." It's not unusual for patrons to sit down in the morning to bowls of gumbo or jambalaya, a plate of BBQ Spaghetti, or a dish of catfish—fried golden—and potatoes. Of course, there's plenty of the more traditional breakfast fare: fat buttermilk biscuits awash in sausage gravy, plate-sized fluffy pancakes, thick strips of grilled bacon, homemade granola, and every kind of omelet that you can think of. Even the oatmeal is surprisingly popular—locally grown and milled by the Vermont Cereal Company in nearby Cabot—topped with fruit and nuts. Lunch follows the same lines, except there are salads served at lunch (Fried Chicken Salad with Buttermilk Dressing is a favorite). Sometimes in the summer River Run is open for dinner. Barbecue is a particular specialty, and locals report developing cravings around mid-March for ribs and collards.

In the past, River Run has hosted "guest chef" nights, bringing in people from the community to cook their specialties. Guest chefs have included Kathy Kilcourse, former owner of the hardware store in town, who cooked up a batch of tasty Szechuan dishes; Margaret Valdez, who re-created her family's Mexican specialties; and Ben Cohen, of Ben & Jerry's fame, who put the fry vat to the test making fried ice cream balls. For a while Steve Bogart—who now runs the extremely popular A Single Pebble restaurant in nearby Berlin—had his wok set up in the waitress station and took over each evening when Jimmy left for the day, the scent of stir-fried garlic and ginger overpowering the scent of barbecue sauce and bacon for a few hours.

In nice weather, patrons—and their kids and their dogs—gather on the porch, reading newspapers and exchanging local gossip. The community bulletin board that hangs outside is full of announcements for yoga classes, used Saabs and pickup trucks, hay for sale, lost dogs and cats, writers' group meetings, apartment rentals, futon couches, and secondhand farm equipment.

Inside, the restaurant seats twenty-four people at mismatched wooden tables surrounded by mismatched wooden chairs.

Expect a wait.

ABOUT THIS BOOK

River Run is successful for two reasons: the food and the atmosphere. We've tried to capture both in this book.

Our food is pretty basic, filling and delicious; the accent, like Jimmy's, is decidedly Southern. The quantities are large; the idea is to share. You can easily halve almost every recipe, but we think you'll be happier if you don't. We think that great leftovers are one of the best reasons to cook great food, and we've tried to give you help on keeping and freezing as many of the dishes as possible.

River Run's atmosphere is relaxed—sometimes rowdy, always lively. If that's the way you like to entertain, then this book is for you.

The recipes here are precise—all tested in home kitchens by home cooks—and will lead to great results. But we see them more as guidelines than formulas. We hope that readers will use their imagination and their taste buds as they cook, and enjoy food, family, and friends in the true spirit of River Run.

INGREDIENTS AND EQUIPMENT

River Run food—and Southern food in general—depends on simple, everyday ingredients. Likewise, the techniques Jimmy uses are pretty basic. But we would like to offer some notes for the home cook.

For example, the word "chop" is used throughout these recipes to designate the cutting of ingredients into pieces ranging in size from ¼ to ½ inch. The idea, generally, is to cut all the similar ingredients (vegetables, for example) in any given recipe about the same size so that they cook in more or less the same time. Sometimes a recipe will instruct you to "mince" an ingredient (usually garlic), and that, of course means to chop it very fine.

Ingredients

As for ingredients, here are some guidelines:

Butter: These recipes all call for unsalted butter. If you use salted butter instead, you may want to reduce the amount of salt in the ingredients list.

Oil: For frying, we prefer canola oil, but you can substitute any vegetable oil. (Many Southerners prefer peanut oil for frying catfish and for most deep-frying.) Be careful with olive oil, though: it burns at a much lower temperature than other vegetable oils.

Flour: Although Southern cooks often use self-rising flour, Jimmy uses all-purpose flour in all but one of these recipes. We like King Arthur unbleached all-purpose flour, not just because King Arthur is an old Vermont company, but because they make an excellent product. The King Arthur catalog, in fact, is one of the best baking catalogs around. You can order flour and kitchen items from it; call (800) 777–4434. Do not sift the flour unless instructed to do so.

Chocolate: Our primary bakers, Nicole Graves and Nessa Rabin, use high-quality imported chocolate in their recipes. But all of them have been successfully tested with Baker's chocolate. Use the imported brands if your budget allows.

Maple Syrup: We hear that states other than Vermont produce maple syrup, but it's hard for us to believe. But no matter where it comes from, use only the pure stuff (see page 47 for a discussion of syrup grades). Don't bother trying to substitute a "maple-flavored" syrup for the real thing.

Oatmeal: Our oatmeal is very popular, mostly because it is made with Eric & Andy's Homegrown Organic Rolled Oats from the Vermont Cereal Co. in Cabot, Vermont. To order, contact the company at 370 Bolton Road, Cabot, VT 05647; tollfree 888-462-8632; www.vermontcereal.com.

Stock: Of course, homemade stock is preferable to canned broth, but sometimes you just don't have any on hand, and a shortcut is welcome. Don't be afraid to substitute canned broth or, in a pinch, water and bouillon. Vegetable base is available in supermarkets and health-food stores, and fish bouillon is on most supermarket shelves. You may, of course, choose to use homemade stocks in these recipes: Any standard cookbook will tell you how to make them.

Beans: Many people like canned beans because of their convenience, but Jimmy is not a fan—he doesn't care much for their texture or taste. Most of the recipes in this book call for using uncooked dried beans. Soak them overnight or use the quick-soak method described in these pages. If you're desperate for time, of course, no one is going to holler too loud if you substitute canned beans.

Tomatoes: We often find ourselves making soups and stews in the winter, when good fresh tomatoes are either not available or are just too expensive. In these cases, canned whole or crushed tomatoes work perfectly. Some recipes call for restaurant-sized #10 cans, which can be found in most supermarkets, but you can substitute four 28-ounce cans instead. Salads and a few other dishes demand plump, ripe, fresh tomatoes; don't bother making them if the produce is inferior.

Garlic: We don't apologize for using garlic powder, and you shouldn't either. Garlic powder is a staple of the Southern pantry and is called for in some dishes. Fresh garlic is used in others.

Eggs: All recipes were tested with Grade A large eggs.

Hot Sauce: You can use your favorite hot sauce, but we prefer our own River Run-Hush Your Mouth Hot Sauce. It, and other condiments—Jimmy's Tupelo Barbecue Sauce, Mother Maya's Red Tomato Ketchup, Don't Be Shy Green Tomato Ketchup and Breakfastlunchanddinner Garlic Sauce—are available from: River Run, P.O. Box 10, Plainfield, VT 05667; (802)863-0499 (phone); (802)863-0377 (fax); or www.riverrunsoul.com.

Salt and Pepper: If possible, use kosher or other coarse salt, and grind your own pepper. If you are feeling lazy or the recipe calls for a large amount of black pepper, use coarsely ground pepper, available in the spice section of the grocery store.

Fish: Fish and fishing are a big part of Jimmy's life, so he tends to cook fish quite a bit and has included some of his favorite recipes here.

• *Catfish*: While bass is his favorite fish to catch, catfish is, by far, his favorite to cook and eat. Farm-raised catfish is big business these days, with

Jimmy's home state, Mississippi, producing about 80 percent of the nation's supply. When shopping, look for fillets that are firm and white, with a sweet, fresh smell. You can substitute catfish in almost any recipe calling for fish or seafood. Also, catfish is high in protein and low in cholesterol. And, by the way, catfish are subsurface feeders, not bottom feeders.

• *Crawfish*: If you don't live in the South—where farm-raised live crawfish are readily available—chances are you will be buying precooked crawfish meat. Make sure you don't overcook it when adding it to soups or stews. Even if live crawfish are available, cooking them up and picking out the tail meat is a time-consuming business when you need a couple of pounds of meat for a single recipe. Save the live crawfish for an old-fashioned crawfish boil, when picking out the meat and sucking the heads is half the fun. But if you are making a soup or stew, use precooked. If it is not available, substitute small shrimp.

• *Shrimp*: I use 21–25 count shrimp for most all recipes. However, if you substitute shrimp for crawfish use 50–60 count.

Meat and Fowl: Most of the recipes here call for common cuts of beef, pork, and chicken. But if you hunt or know someone who does, you can add or substitute almost any kind of game or wild fowl in many of these recipes: venison, squirrel, duck, dove, quail, grouse, turkey, or rabbit. (You can also buy decent farm-raised game.) When it comes to sausage, andouille sausage—the spicy, smoked pork sausage that is a staple of Cajun cooking—is our choice; if you can't find it, substitute another smoked pork sausage, like kielbasa.

Equipment

Even though River Run has a professional kitchen, the equipment—with the exception of the fry vat—is not much different from what you have at home. All these recipes have been tested in a home kitchen.

Dutch Oven and Cast-Iron Skillet: Two essentials, called for repeatedly in these recipes and in constant use at River Run. The Dutch oven can be used not only for soups and stews but for deep-frying.

Baking Parchment: Useful for lining cookie sheets.

Electric Mixer: A fancy heavy-duty mixer is nice, but a plain handheld one will work too.

Food Processor: In most recipes, you can use a blender instead, or just a good knife.

Long-Handled Whisk: You will find a whisk ideal for stirring a roux and for lots of other tasks as well.

Cooking Thermometers: A deep-fry/candy thermometer will help you in two ways: first, it lets you know when the oil is hot enough for frying; and second, it helps you regulate the heat under the pot so that the temperature of the oil stays steady. An instant-read thermometer is vital for making sure that eggs cooked in a custard reach a safe temperature.

Long Pair of Tongs: Helpful when placing food in and taking it out of hot oil.

CHAPTER 1

SOUPS & STEWS

Vermont is soup country. The cold starts seeping in around October (an August frost is not unheard of), and by deer season (mid-November), if we're lucky, we've had our first snowfall. For a week or so in midwinter, we can count on the temperature plunging to 20 or 30 below at night and "warming up" to zero during the day. Customers, accompanied by frigid blasts of air, come stomping in, wearing huge felt-lined boots and an amazing variety of hats (fleece, wool, felt; store-bought, hand-knit, and many of them one-of-a-kind). At this time of year, tables far from the door are popular. And so are soups and stews. We tend to make our soups very thick and stewlike, and we serve them up in colorful pottery bowls made by Maya's mom, Charlotte Potok, who lives next door to us and who has been our most loyal supporter from the beginning.

The dishes in this chapter tend to be a little time-consuming—they require lots of peeling and chopping. But you'll be rewarded for your efforts with a huge pot of something delicious to feed your friends and family. Most of these dishes keep well, and many are even better when reheated the next day.

BBQ CHICKEN
& RICE SOUP

It's hard to resist serving leftover BBQ Chicken on its own for breakfast the next day. But this recipe gives you an alternative: It makes a tasty and economical lunch or supper.

4 tablespoons (½ stick) unsalted butter
1 medium onion, peeled and chopped (about 1 cup)
1 large carrot, peeled and chopped (about 1 cup)
½ red or green bell pepper, seeded and chopped (about ½ cup)
¼ cup all-purpose flour
6 cups chicken stock or canned broth
2½ to 3 cups shredded BBQ Chicken (page 137)
Salt, to taste
Freshly ground black pepper, to taste
Dry BBQ Rub (page 195), to taste
1 cup chopped fresh parsley
½ cup half-and-half
1 cup uncooked white rice

Melt the butter in a heavy-bottomed pot or Dutch oven set over medium-high heat and, when bubbling, sauté the onion, carrot, and bell pepper until they start to soften, 5 to 7 minutes. (The carrot will still be a little crunchy.) Add the flour and cook, stirring, until it starts to brown, about 4 or 5 minutes more. The flour will stick as it cooks, so scrape the bottom of the pot a bit.

3

Add the stock (or broth) and shredded chicken. Season with salt, pepper, and rub. Reduce the heat to keep the soup on a low simmer, and add the parsley and half-and-half. Be careful not to let the soup boil. Add the rice and let cook, with the pot mostly covered, until the rice is tender, about 20 to 30 minutes.

Serve immediately.

Yield: 6 to 8 servings

BUTTER BEAN SOUP

If you live in the South, you get butter beans; in the rest of the country, you get limas. "Butter beans" is, in truth, another name for lima beans, but the name refers to fresh, tender, tiny limas. Speckled butter beans—dotted with dark purplish spots—have the shortest growing season and are considered by many to be the most flavorful. This soup works best with fresh, tiny butter beans (speckled if you can get 'em), but regular frozen limas will work too.

5 tablespoons unsalted butter
1½ medium onions, peeled and chopped (about 1½ cups)
1 large carrot, peeled and chopped (about 1 cup)
⅓ cup all-purpose flour
8 cups chicken or vegetable stock or canned broth
2 pounds fresh or frozen baby lima beans
1 teaspoon dried tarragon
1 teaspoon dried thyme
1 teaspoon dried oregano
2 cups half-and-half
Salt, to taste
Freshly ground black pepper, to taste

Melt the butter in a heavy-bottomed pot or Dutch oven set over medium-high heat and, when bubbling, sauté the onions and carrot until

they start to soften, 5 to 7 minutes. (The carrot will still be a little crunchy.) Stir in the flour and cook until it starts to brown, another 4 or 5 minutes. The flour will stick as it cooks, so scrape the bottom of the pot a bit.

Add the stock (or broth), limas, tarragon, thyme, and oregano and bring to a boil. Turn the heat off and add the half-and-half. Season with salt and pepper.

Puree about half the soup in a food processor or blender until quite smooth. Return it to the soup pot. Heat through and serve.

Yield: 8 to 10 servings

Paul Reed, psychotherapist;
Alex Halasz, teacher;
and Lianna Reed.

ANNA'S PEANUT SOUP

Anna Noel Woolf, from Demopolis, Alabama, worked for us for some time as a waitress and cook. She really mastered the art of soup making: "My soups evolved as the fridge emptied," she says. This soup is one of our most requested. We tend to serve it in cup-sized servings because it is so rich and creamy.

4 tablespoons (½ stick) unsalted butter
1 small stalk celery, trimmed and
    chopped (about ½ cup)
½ medium onion, peeled and chopped
    (about ½ cup)
1 small carrot, peeled and chopped
    (about ½ cup)
¼ cup all-purpose flour
¼ cup dry white wine
1 quart chicken stock or canned broth
1 bay leaf
½ teaspoon dried tarragon
1 cup smooth peanut butter
1½ cups heavy cream or half-and-half
1 teaspoon hot sauce, or more to taste
Salt, to taste
Freshly ground black pepper, to taste
Toasted sesame seeds, for garnish (optional)

Anna Woolf.

7

Melt the butter in a heavy-bottomed pot or Dutch oven set over medium-high heat and, when bubbling, sauté the celery, onion, and carrot until soft and beginning to brown, 10 to 12 minutes. Add the flour and cook, stirring, for a few minutes. The flour will stick as it cooks, so scrape the bottom of the pot a bit. Add the wine and cook, continuing to scrape, for a few minutes.

Add the stock (or broth), bay leaf, and tarragon and bring to a boil. As soon as the soup boils, remove the pot from the heat, discard the bay leaf, and scoop out the vegetables with a slotted spoon into the bowl of a food processor or blender. Add a bit of the broth from the pot to the vegetables and puree until fairly smooth. Return the puree to the pot, return the pot to the heat, and adjust the heat to low. Stir in the peanut butter, a bit at a time, then whisk until smooth. Add the cream (or half-and-half) and hot sauce. Season with salt and pepper.

Serve immediately, topped with toasted sesame seeds, if desired.

Yield: about 8 servings

BLACK BEAN SOUP

This is a basic, hearty, main-course soup. Serve it with a salad and good bread, and you've got yourself a meal.

1 pound dried black beans

5 strips thick-cut lean smoked bacon, chopped

Butter, if needed

2 medium onions, peeled and chopped (about 2 cups)

4 small stalks celery, trimmed and chopped (about 2 cups)

2 fresh jalapeño peppers, stemmed, seeded and chopped

3 cloves garlic, peeled and minced

4 to 6 cups chicken stock or canned broth

½ cup slightly sweet table wine (a blush or white Zinfandel is good)

2 pounds fresh tomatoes or one 28-ounce can whole tomatoes, drained

Fresh or dried herbs—oregano, thyme, and basil—to taste (about 1 tablespoon fresh or 2 teaspoons dried, total)

Hot sauce, to taste

Salt, to taste

Freshly ground black pepper, to taste

Cider or balsamic vinegar, for serving (optional)

Chopped fresh cilantro, seeded and chopped jalapeño peppers, shredded Monterey Jack or cheddar cheese, plain yogurt or sour cream, for garnish (optional)

The night before you are going to cook the soup, rinse the beans and pick them over, discarding any small stones or funny-looking beans. Soak the beans overnight in enough cold water to cover by several inches.

The next morning, drain the beans. Return them to the pot, cover them with several inches of water again, and bring the pot to a boil. Reduce to a simmer and cook until the beans are tender (this usually takes about an hour, but the time depends on the age of the beans). Drain the beans and set them aside.

If you have forgotten to soak the beans overnight or don't have the time, use the quick-soak method: Prepare the beans as above, but instead of soaking them overnight, bring them to a boil. Boil for 2 minutes, shut off the heat, and let the beans sit for about an hour. Drain them and proceed to cook as above.

Line a plate with paper towels.

Fry the bacon until almost crisp in a heavy-duty skillet. Set the bacon aside on the lined plate to drain. Pour the bacon fat into a heavy-bottomed soup pot—you want about 3 tablespoons. Discard any excess. If there is not enough, add butter to make 3 tablespoons.

Heat the bacon fat (and butter, if needed) and sauté the onions, celery, and jalapeños until soft, about 10 minutes. Add the garlic and cook a few more minutes. Add the cooked beans, 4 cups of stock (or broth), wine, tomatoes, herbs, and a few dashes of hot sauce. Simmer over very low heat, with the pot mostly covered, for about 30 minutes; add more stock if the soup looks too thick. Add the crumbled bacon and cook about 15 minutes longer. Season with salt and pepper.

Ladle into bowls and serve immediately. Or add a teaspoon of vinegar to each serving to bring out the flavors. If desired, serve with some or all of the suggested garnishes.

Yield: 6 to 8 servings

RED BEANS & RICE SOUP

This soup seemed like the obvious answer to leftover red beans and rice. Now we often skip making plain red beans and rice, and go right to the soup.

1 pound dried red beans (to make 6 cups cooked)
2 cups uncooked white rice (to make 6 cups cooked)
5 strips thick-cut lean smoked bacon, chopped
2 medium onions, peeled and chopped (about 2 cups)
3 small carrots, peeled and chopped (about 1½ cups)
12 cups chicken stock or canned broth
4 bay leaves
Salt, to taste
Freshly ground black pepper, to taste
Generous pinch ground cumin
Generous pinch chili powder
4 tablespoons chopped fresh basil, or 2 tablespoons dried
2 to 4 tablespoons heavy cream (optional)
Hot sauce, for serving

The night before you are going to cook the soup, rinse the beans and pick them over, discarding any small stones or funny-looking beans. Soak the beans overnight in enough cold water to cover by several inches.

The next morning, drain the beans. Return them to the pot, cover them with several inches of water again, and bring the pot to a boil. Reduce to a simmer and cook until the beans are tender (this usually takes about an hour,

11

but the time depends on the age of the beans). Drain the beans and set them aside.

If you have forgotten to soak the beans overnight or don't have the time, use the quick-soak method: Prepare the beans as above, but instead of soaking them overnight, bring them to a boil. Boil for 2 minutes, shut off the heat, and let the beans sit for about an hour. Drain them and proceed to cook as above.

While the beans are cooking, make the rice according to package directions. When done, set aside.

Heat a large pot over medium-high heat. When hot, throw in the chopped bacon. Cook until some of the fat is rendered, then add the onions and carrots. Cook, stirring, until the vegetables are soft, about 10 minutes.

Drain the cooked beans and add them to the pot. Add the stock (or broth), bay leaves, salt and pepper, cumin, chili powder, and basil. Simmer, with the pot mostly covered, about 30 minutes. Taste and add more salt, pepper, cumin or chili powder, if needed.

Add the cooked rice and simmer, uncovered, for 15 more minutes. The soup will thicken slightly. Remove from the heat. Add a splash of heavy cream, if desired; it helps bring the flavors together. Remove the bay leaves as you serve the soup.

Serve, passing around a bottle of hot sauce.

Yield: about 10 servings

SNOW PEA & MUSHROOM SOUP

This is a light, delicate soup; the snow peas—along with the sesame oil and soy sauce—give it a slightly Asian flavor. You can also use sugar snaps or green beans.

2 tablespoons (¼ stick) unsalted butter
½ medium onion, peeled and chopped (about ½ cup)
1 large carrot, peeled and chopped (about 1 cup)
1 small stalk celery, trimmed and chopped (about ½ cup)
2 tablespoons all-purpose flour
5 cups chicken or vegetable stock or canned broth
1½ teaspoons Asian sesame oil (made with toasted sesame seeds)
¾ teaspoon minced fresh ginger
¾ teaspoon minced garlic
¾ teaspoon soy sauce, or more to taste
¼ pound mushrooms (any type—your choice), cleaned and sliced
½ pound snow peas, cut in half
Freshly ground black pepper, to taste

Melt the butter in a saucepan large enough to hold the stock and all the other ingredients. When the butter starts to sizzle, sauté the onion, carrot, and celery until they start to soften, 5 to 7 minutes. The carrots will still be a little crunchy. Add the flour and cook, stirring, until it starts to brown, about 4 or 5 minutes more. The flour will stick as it cooks, so scrape the bottom of the pot a bit.

Add the stock (or broth) and cook until it starts to thicken.

While the soup is cooking, heat the sesame oil in a small skillet. Add the ginger, garlic, and soy sauce and cook, stirring, for a couple of minutes. Add the mushrooms and snow peas and stir-fry for a couple of minutes. Then add all of this to the soup and heat through.

Season with pepper, taste and, if needed, add more soy sauce.

Yield: 4 to 6 servings

Aron Steward, student.

14

VEGGIE SOUP

Marialisa's mother and aunt—Diana and Antoinette Calta—have been making this delicious vegetable-packed soup for years. It serves a lot of people, keeps for quite a few days, and tastes even better a day or two after it's been made. Furthermore, you can add almost anything to it: pumpkin or acorn squash, rice or barley, or what have you. In other words, it's got "River Run" written all over it.

1 large onion
3 cloves garlic
2 large stalks celery, leafy tops included
¼ medium head green cabbage
1 medium head escarole, or 1 pound spinach
¼ cup olive oil
10 cups beef stock, canned broth, or broth made with beef bouillon or
    vegetable soup base
3 large potatoes
3 medium turnips
2 large carrots
One 28-ounce can whole tomatoes, with juice
Two 15½-ounce cans kidney beans, drained and rinsed
½ cup chopped fresh parsley
4 tablespoons (½ stick) unsalted butter

Peel and chop the onion (you should have about 1½ cups). Do the same to the garlic. Trim the tough ends off the celery, but leave any leafy greens on top.

Chop the stalks (and leafy parts) into a medium dice (you should have a scant 2 cups). Shred the cabbage (you should have about 3 cups). Remove and discard the tough outer leaves of the escarole (or if using spinach, trim and discard the stems). Chop the escarole (or spinach) quite finely (you should have about 8 cups). Rinse the escarole (or spinach) and cabbage, but do not drain them too well—some of the water should still be on the leaves.

Hannah Van Susternen, Antoinette, and Diana Calta.

Heat the oil in a large soup pot until hot. Add the onion, garlic, celery, cabbage, and escarole (or spinach). Cover and simmer, stirring every once in a while, until the greens are wilted.

Meanwhile, heat the stock (or broth) until boiling. Peel the potatoes, turnips, and carrots. Cut the turnips and carrots into ¾-inch dice (you'll have 3 to 4 cups turnips and about 2 cups carrots).

When the greens are wilted, put the whole potatoes and diced turnips and carrots in the pot. Cover them with the boiling stock. Simmer, with the pot mostly covered, until the potatoes are tender.

Remove the potatoes from the pot with a slotted spoon. In a bowl, mash 2 of the potatoes and return them to the pot. Cut the remaining cooked potato into small chunks and put back in the soup.

Add the canned tomatoes with their juice, and stir, chopping the tomatoes with your spoon as you stir. Add the beans and parsley. Cook, mostly covered, for about 20 minutes.

Just before serving, stir in the butter.

Yield: 12 to 14 servings

SUMMER SQUASH SOUP

We have a small garden at home and grow as many vegetables as we can for River Run. We always seem to have an abundance of squash, and we've found that a nice, fresh soup is a very good way to use them up.

    4 medium yellow summer squash, peeled, halved, and seeded
    Salt, to taste
    Freshly ground black pepper, to taste
    2 tablespoons (¼ stick) unsalted butter
    2 medium onions, peeled and chopped (about 2 cups)
    4 cups chicken or vegetable stock or canned broth
    1 teaspoon ground cumin
    1 teaspoon curry powder
    ½ teaspoon ground cinnamon
    1 cup half-and-half
    Minced red bell pepper, finely chopped carrot, or toasted sesame
        seeds, for garnish (optional)

Set the oven to 375 degrees.

Sprinkle the squash with salt and pepper to taste, and bake for about 30 minutes or until the squash just starts to soften. Remove, allow to cool, and cut into 1-inch pieces.

Melt the butter in a large soup pot and sauté the onions. When they start to soften and turn brown (10 to 12 minutes), add the squash, stock (or broth) and spices. Bring the soup to a boil, remove from the heat, and let cool.

Ann Turner and Katie Harrington.

When it has cooled a bit, puree it in a food processor or blender.

Return the pureed soup to the pot; taste for salt and pepper. Add the half-and-half and cook over medium heat until it is good and hot but not boiling.

Serve plain or topped with some or all of the suggested garnishes.

Yield: about 6 servings

VERMONT GAZPACHO

This recipe came to us from Benjamin Cevelo, executive chef at the Boston Museum of Fine Arts. Chef Benjamin created this gazpacho during his Vermont days, when he was a teacher at the Essex, Vermont, campus of the New England Culinary Institute. This soup packs a wallop, thanks to incredibly fresh flavors and a dose of Asian chili paste or hot sauce.

1 large ear fresh corn, husked, or 1¼ cups frozen corn kernels

2 tablespoons olive oil

1 clove garlic, peeled and minced

½ medium red onion, peeled and chopped (about ¾ cup)

1 shallot, peeled and minced

½ large cucumber, peeled, seeded, and chopped (about 1 cup)

½ red bell pepper, seeded and chopped (about ½ cup)

½ yellow bell pepper, seeded and chopped (about ½ cup)

½ green bell pepper, seeded and chopped (about ½ cup)

6 plum tomatoes, roughly chopped (about 2½ cups)

One 28-ounce can whole tomatoes, with juice

2 tablespoons chopped fresh cilantro

2 tablespoons fresh, chopped basil leaves

1 to 2 tablespoons Asian chili paste or hot sauce

2 tablespoons red wine vinegar

1 tablespoon honey

1 tablespoon orange juice

1 tablespoon Asian sesame oil (made with toasted sesame seeds)

Asian chili paste or hot sauce, for serving (optional)

Chopped fresh cilantro, for garnish (optional)

If using fresh corn, steam it for a few minutes. When cool enough to handle, cut a thin slice off the fat end of the cob and stand it in a shallow bowl. With a sharp knife, cut the corn off the cob. (If using frozen corn, cook it according to package directions; drain well.) Put the corn in the bowl of a food processor fitted with a metal blade.

In a skillet set over medium-high heat, heat the oil. Sauté the garlic, onion, and shallot until soft, 7 to 10 minutes. Using a rubber spatula, scrape the sautéed mixture into the bowl of the food processor.

Add the cucumber, bell peppers, fresh and canned tomatoes (and juice), cilantro, basil, chili paste (or hot sauce), vinegar, honey, orange juice, and sesame oil to the food processor. Pulse until well blended. Chill. Taste and adjust seasonings, as needed.

Serve with extra chili paste or hot sauce and additional chopped cilantro, if desired.

Yield: 6 to 8 servings

STRAWBERRY SOUP

Vermont has lots of small farms that produce terrific strawberries each year, and we are always looking for ways to use them. This recipe comes to us from Rhea Wilson, a writer and editor, loyal customer, and terrific home cook. Made in early summer, when strawberries are at their peak, it is amazing, but it can also be made in the winter—with only slightly lesser results—with frozen strawberries. It is only slightly sweet; we serve it—very cold—as a first course, but it also makes an interesting dessert soup. Years ago Rhea made a huge batch of it for her daughter Jemma's bat mitzvah, and so she calls it "Jemma's Famous Bat Mitzvah Soup."

Rhea Wilson.

3 cups fresh strawberries, hulled and rinsed, or
    frozen strawberries (see note)
½ cup sugar
½ cup sour cream
1½ cups ice water
½ cup chilled dry white wine

    Put all the ingredients in a blender and puree until smooth. Cover and chill very thoroughly before serving.

    Note: If using frozen strawberries, use only 1 cup water. You will not have to chill the soup if you serve it immediately.

    Yield: about 4 servings

MAKING A ROUX

A roux is one of the most important elements of Cajun/Creole cooking. (The word comes from the Old French *rous*, for reddish brown.) It is, very simply, equal parts of fat and flour cooked until it is anywhere from light brown to almost black—depending on what you are using it for. A good rule of thumb is to make a light roux for dark meats and a dark roux for light meats and seafood.

While a roux is used to thicken dishes, it also adds a distinctive deep, nutty flavor to the food. It is an essential part of étouffée, stews, and soups. In this book, you will need to make a nice dark roux for Gumbo (page 24) and a medium roux for Tiny's Sauce Picante (page 27). Lots of other recipes—for gravies and stews—require you to cook fat and flour together for a short period of time, which is the beginning of a roux.

Jimmy always looks forward to making a roux, probably because the foods that require one are the foods he loves best. At any rate, it's a lot of fun and a challenging part of cooking.

Jimmy first learned how to make a roux the old way—cooking the mixture over medium heat for an hour or more. This method is safe: you won't burn the roux and you do not have to stir it every single second. But it does take a long time.

In his cookbooks chef Paul Prudhomme describes a much quicker method: he heats the oil until it is smoking and gradually but quickly adds the flour while stirring with a long-handled whisk. His method takes only 5 to 10 minutes.

Jimmy uses a combination of the old and the new methods and can produce a good, dark roux in 15 to 20 minutes.

Here are his directions: Heat the oil (Jimmy prefers canola) in a Dutch oven until it just starts to smoke. Add an equal measure of flour, a bit at a time, whisking (a long-handled whisk works best) all the while. Within a few minutes the flour will be incorporated and the color of milk chocolate. If you need a dark roux, keep cooking—whisking continually—even if it seems to be burning. You can lower the heat a little bit, but the real trick is to keep whisking. A dark roux should be the color of bittersweet chocolate; when done, it will be almost black and about the consistency of cake frosting.

A roux is not difficult to master; it requires patience and courage more than any special talent. Keep practicing until you get the hang of it.

GUMBO

One of our favorite combinations for gumbo is crawfish and andouille sausage, which is the recipe given here. As substitutions, kielbasa and small (50/60 count) shrimp work fine; in fact, you can substitute chicken, beef, pork, seafood, game, or vegetables in just about any combination that suits you. Use the lesser amount of cayenne if using a spicy sausage like andouille; use more if using blander meats or if you like your gumbo real, real hot.

2 medium onions, peeled and chopped (about 2 cups)
1½ medium green bell peppers, seeded and chopped (about 1½ cups)
2 small stalks celery, trimmed and chopped (about 1 cup)
2 tablespoons chopped garlic
1 tablespoon salt
1 tablespoon coarsely ground black pepper
1 tablespoon white pepper
½ to 1 tablespoon cayenne pepper
1 tablespoon dried thyme
1½ teaspoons dried oregano
1½ teaspoons dried basil
1 cup canola oil
1 cup all-purpose flour, or more if needed
7 cups stock, preferably fish stock, or broth made with fish bouillon
    (chicken will do)
1 pound andouille sausage, sliced
2 pounds crawfish meat
9 cups cooked white rice

It's always a good idea to get everything good and ready before you start any recipe, but that's especially true with this one. Mix the chopped vegetables and garlic together. Measure and combine the salt, spices, and herbs. Measure out the oil and flour, keeping extra flour handy if you need it for thickening. Put the stock in a big soup pot.

Now, in a skillet, brown the sausage (or meat or game of your choosing). Remove the sausage with a slotted spoon and set it aside.

The next step is to make the roux (page 22). Heat the oil in a Dutch oven over very high heat. When it just starts to smoke, start adding the flour, a few tablespoons at a time, whisking constantly. Adjust the heat to medium-high. Whisk constantly—a long-handled whisk works best—until the roux reaches a very dark brown, almost black color (think of the color of dark chocolate). If it is not thickening up, add a little more flour. This whole process will take 15 to 20 minutes; you may think the roux is burned and ruined, but this is how it is supposed to look.

When the roux is nice and dark and thick (the consistency of cake frosting), turn off the heat and add the vegetables and spice mix. Continue whisking for a few more minutes. Set the Dutch oven aside.

Heat the stock until it reaches a boil. Add the roux-vegetable mixture to the boiling stock, stirring with a whisk or long-handled spoon. When all of the roux has been added, put the pot on a low boil and, while stirring, add the cooked sausage. Stir well, reduce the heat, and simmer for about ½ hour, with the pot mostly covered.

If you are using crawfish meat, it is probably precooked, so add it and cook just enough to warm it through. If using shrimp, shell it, add to the pot, and cook until just done, about 3 to 5 minutes (do not overcook). Serve over a mound of rice in deep dinner plates or large bowls.

Gumbo will keep for several days, covered, in the refrigerator, and does

not suffer from reheating. If, after serving it the first time, you wind up with more leftover "gravy" than meat or fish, just add some more cooked meat or seafood (poached chicken is easy and works well) to extend your gumbo for another meal.

Yield: 8 to 10 servings

Gregg Bradley, "River Run's right-hand man." Although Gregg doesn't officially work at River Run he is always willing to help out: running errands, fixing things, washing dishes—whatever he can do. Even if it's just holding the refrigerator up and watching us work.

Keith Heard, Jimmy Kennedy, Tiny Heard, Doug Curtiss,
Homer Jolly, and Skipper Davis.

TINY'S SAUCE PICANTE

Even though this is called a "sauce," it is really a kind of stew—you eat it in a
bowl over rice. The recipe comes to River Run by way of our good friend Tiny
Heard, of Brooksville, Mississippi. Tiny has been a big influence on Jimmy's
cooking and a source of information about many River Run recipes, especially
BBQ. Jimmy always looks forward to the chance to do some cooking with
Tiny, whether it be a hog-roasting for several hundred or breakfast for the
"Cloudy Brothers," a group of their friends who get together in Vermont late
in the winter to cook, eat, and occasionally ski or ice-fish.

Tiny is proud of this family recipe, which comes—via his grandparents—
from the bayou country of south Louisiana. "It lasted because it's easy and

inexpensive, just right for the hard times it came out of," says Tiny. The basic recipe here calls for chicken, but Tiny often makes it with duck, dove, shrimp, crab, turtle, or smoked sausage, alone or in combination. He likes to throw in a few oysters at the last minute as well. "Use your imagination," says Tiny, "and it will be good."

1½ cups all-purpose flour, plus more if needed
1 teaspoon salt, plus more if needed
1 teaspoon freshly ground black pepper, plus more if needed
1 whole frying chicken (3 to 4 pounds), cut up, or 3 to 4 pounds
   thighs or legs
2 tablespoons canola oil, plus more if needed
One 15-ounce can tomato sauce, with juice
Three 14½-ounce cans chicken broth
3 medium onions, peeled and chopped (about 3 cups)
1 bunch green onions, trimmed and chopped
6 cups cooked white rice

Mix 1 cup of the flour with a teaspoon each of salt and pepper in a shallow bowl. Dredge the chicken pieces in the seasoned flour until well coated.

In a heavy-bottomed pot or Dutch oven, heat the oil over medium-high heat. Working in batches, brown the chicken, turning the pieces as you cook. When browned, remove them from the pot and set them aside on a plate. Keep the pot on the heat.

Now you will make a medium roux (page 22). You should have about ½ cup drippings in the pot—you can eyeball the amount or measure it. If you don't have enough, add some canola oil to make ½ cup. Add an equal amount of flour, a bit at a time, stirring constantly until the mixture is a medium brown color

28

(this will take somewhere between 5 and 10 minutes). Add the tomatoes (and juice), broth, onions, green onions, and browned chicken, along with any drippings that have accumulated on the plate. (Note: If you don't have any chicken broth, fill the empty tomato can with water 3 times and add to the pot.) Reduce the heat until the stew is simmering. Cook, with the pot mostly covered, until the chicken is cooked through and tender, about 45 minutes to an hour (cut into a piece to make sure it isn't pink inside). Taste and add salt and pepper, if needed.

Serve over cooked rice.

Yield: about 6 servings

CHILI

This thick, meaty chili is on the mild side, and while it is delicious right out of the pot, it's even better the next day. It also can be frozen for several months if well wrapped.

- 1 pound dried beans: Great Northern, pinto, white, garbanzo, or any combination (to make about 6 cups cooked)
- 2 pounds ground beef
- 3 pounds cubed meat: pork, venison, or chicken
- 2 large onions, peeled and chopped (about 2½ cups)
- 2 large green bell peppers, seeded and chopped (about 2½ cups)
- 6 cloves garlic, peeled and minced
- 3 tablespoons chili powder
- 1 tablespoon ground cumin
- 1 tablespoon dried oregano
- Salt, to taste
- Freshly ground black pepper, to taste
- Two 12-ounce bottles of beer
- 1 to 2 cups beef stock or canned broth, if needed
- 4 pounds fresh or canned tomatoes, chopped (if canned, drain juice)
- Two 6-ounce cans tomato paste
- Grated cheddar or Monterey Jack or sour cream, for serving

The night before you are going to cook the chili, rinse the beans and pick them over, discarding any small stones or funny-looking beans. Soak the beans overnight in enough cold water to cover by several inches.

The next morning, drain the beans. Return them to the pot, cover them with several inches of water again, and bring the pot to a boil. Reduce to a simmer and cook until the beans are tender (this usually takes about an hour, but the time depends on the age of the beans). Drain the beans and set them aside.

If you have forgotten to soak the beans overnight or don't have the time, use the quick-soak method: Prepare the beans as above, but instead of soaking them overnight, bring them to a boil. Boil for 2 minutes, shut off the heat, and let the beans sit for about an hour. Drain them and proceed to cook as above.

Heat a large, heavy pot or Dutch oven over medium-high heat. Add the ground beef and brown until it is cooked through. Remove it with a slotted spoon and then brown the cubed meat in the drippings. Remove the meat cubes with a slotted spoon and drain most of the drippings off, leaving 2 or 3 tablespoons. Add the onions, peppers, and garlic and sauté until they are soft, about 7 to 10 minutes.

Return both meats to the pot and add the chili powder, cumin, oregano, salt, and pepper. Add both bottles of beer. If the mixture is not covered with liquid, add enough beef stock (or broth) to cover. Adjust the heat to bring the mixture to a slow boil and, when it is just boiling, add the tomatoes and tomato paste. Return to a boil and then lower the heat and simmer, with the pot mostly covered, for at least 2 to 3 hours (the longer, the better). Add the cooked beans the last half hour. Taste and adjust the seasonings.

Serve with grated cheese or sour cream.

Yield: 16 to 20 servings

PINE BARK STEW

From what we understand, pine bark stew could very well be the official state dish of South Carolina. The name is said to have evolved during the Revolutionary War, when patriots hiding in the South Carolina swamps were forced to eat their fish stew on plates made of pine bark. At River Run we find a soup bowl works too.

½ pound thick-cut lean smoked bacon, chopped
2 medium onions, peeled and chopped (about 2 cups)
2 quarts fish stock or broth made with fish bouillon
3 medium-large potatoes, scrubbed and cut into 1-inch pieces
   (2 to 3 cups)
One 28-ounce canned chopped or crushed tomatoes, with juice
One 6-ounce can tomato paste
¼ cup white vinegar
½ teaspoon ground cinnamon
1 tablespoon sugar
2 pounds catfish fillets, cut into 1-inch pieces
Salt, to taste
Freshly ground black pepper, to taste

Line a plate with paper towels.

In a skillet, cook the bacon until crisp. Remove with slotted spoon and drain on the lined plate. Discard all but about 1 tablespoon of the bacon grease.

Sauté the onions in the bacon grease until they begin to soften, about 5 to 7 minutes. Remove from the skillet with a slotted spoon and set aside.

In a large soup pot, heat the fish stock (or broth). Add the potatoes, bring to a low boil, and cook until almost done, 6 to 8 minutes. Now add the tomatoes (and juice), tomato paste, vinegar, cinnamon, sugar, and cooked bacon and onions. Stir well and cook, uncovered, at a low simmer for 10 to 15 minutes.

Add the catfish and cook, with the pot mostly covered, until it is done, about 10 to 15 minutes. Taste for seasoning, adding salt and pepper as needed.

Yield: about 8 servings

Albert St.Cyr. Since Jimmy first moved to Plainfield, he began to hear stories about Albert—all of them good of course.

SEAFOOD STEW

This recipe came from Maya's mom, Charlotte. She gets the credit for the salmon, mussels, and scallops; Jimmy threw in the catfish for a little Mississippi flavor.

2 tablespoons (¼ stick) unsalted butter

1 medium onion, peeled and chopped (about 1 cup)

1 medium red bell pepper, seeded and chopped (about 1 cup)

½ a large bulb fennel, trimmed and chopped (about 1 cup)

One 15½-ounce can whole tomatoes, with juice

1 pound fresh ripe tomatoes, stemmed and chopped

2 cups fish stock or broth made with fish bouillon

1 cup dry white wine

2 or more cups water

2 to 4 cloves garlic, peeled and chopped

20 to 30 toasted almonds, roughly chopped

½ cup minced fresh parsley

2 egg yolks

4 tablespoons olive oil

1 teaspoon hot sauce, or more to taste

Salt, to taste

Freshly ground black pepper, to taste

1 pound catfish fillets, cut into bite-sized pieces

1 pound salmon fillets, cut into bite-sized pieces

2 pounds mussels, "beards" removed, rinsed under
    cold running water (discard any open mussels)
1 pound shrimp (21/25 count), peeled
½ pound shucked scallops

In a heavy-bottomed pot or Dutch oven, melt the butter over medium-high heat. When bubbling, sauté the onion, bell pepper, and fennel until they are fairly soft, 10 to 12 minutes. Add the canned and fresh tomatoes, fish stock (or broth), wine, and water and cook, with the pot mostly covered, for 30 minutes.

Barry Goldensohn, poet and professor;
Lorrie Goldensohn, poet and scholar.

While the stew is cooking, grind or blend the garlic, almonds, parsley, egg yolks, olive oil, and hot sauce until smooth in a mini-food processor or blender. Stir the pureed mixture into the stew and season with salt and pepper. Add all the fish except the shrimp and scallops. Cook until the mussels open. Add the shrimp and cook until they are turning pink. Add the scallops and cook until they are just opaque and heated through (don't overcook). Discard any unopened mussels before serving.

Serve immediately.

Yield: 10 to 12 servings

CHAPTER 2

FRITTERS, GRIDDLE CAKES, BREADS & CEREAL

Many of the foods in this chapter are traditional treats like pancakes, grit cakes, coffee cake, French toast, and biscuits. But don't overlook the okra fritters, corn fritters, and black-eyed pea cakes, which can be served at any meal.

The trick for all these griddle dishes is a good, hot, heavy-duty skillet, a spatula, and some patience. Most fritters and cakes are best left alone to cook: Flipping them from side to side or continually flattening them with the spatula does not produce the best results. Because these foods are not deep-fried, a candy/fry thermometer won't help you determine the heat of the oil (the oil won't be deep enough for the thermometer to work). Instead, watch the surface of the oil; when it starts to look wavy, it's ready. Keep an eye on it while cooking: the steadier the temperature, the better the results.

Cooking griddle dishes usually requires that you be at the stove while your guests are enjoying the fruits of your labor. To avoid the short-order-cook syndrome, set your oven to warm, line a baking sheet with a brown paper bag or paper towels, and let the fritters sit in the warm oven while you finish cooking.

A note on bread: Because we run a restaurant, not a bakery, our bread recipes are of the quick and easy variety. When we want great, European-style bread to accompany a soup, stew, or other main dish, we buy it from Jules and Helen Rabin, who own the renowned Upland Bakers, an artisanal bakery right in Plainfield. Our sliced bread—oatmeal, raisin, and white—comes from another excellent bakery, The Manghi's Bread, in nearby Montpelier. But for biscuits, corn bread, tea breads, and the like, we're on our own. And we do a pretty good job of it too.

CORN FRITTERS

We pretty much serve these fritters in the same way we do Grit Cakes (page 43), with eggs and some kind of sauce over them (see Ranchero Sauce, page 177, or Hot Pepper Hollandaise, page 171). They can also be served with a salad for lunch or as a side dish with Fried Catfish (page 121), Fried Chicken (page 109), BBQ Chicken (page 137), Country-Style Spare Ribs (page 136), or Pulled Pork (page 134) for dinner.

3 large ears fresh corn, husked, or 4 cups frozen corn kernels
3½ cups all-purpose flour
½ cup yellow cornmeal
2 tablespoons baking powder
2 teaspoons salt
1 teaspoon freshly ground black pepper
1 teaspoon white pepper
3 cups half-and-half or whole milk
4 eggs
½ cup (total) of any or all of the following: chopped onions, green onions, red bell pepper, jalapeños (optional)
Canola oil, for frying (⅔ to 1½ cups for a 10-inch skillet)

If using fresh corn, steam the ears for a few minutes. When cool enough to handle, cut a thin slice off the fat end of an ear and stand it in a shallow bowl. With a sharp knife, cut the corn off the cob. Repeat for remaining 2 cobs. You should have about 4 cups of kernels. (If using frozen corn, place it in a colander and run hot water over it to thaw; drain well.)

39

Mix the flour, cornmeal, baking powder, salt, black pepper, and white pepper in a large bowl. In another bowl, mix and blend the corn kernels, half-and-half (or milk), and eggs. Add the wet ingredients to the dry ingredients and mix well. If you are adding any of the optional ingredients, mix them in now.

Set the oven to warm. Line a baking sheet with a brown paper bag or paper towels.

Heat ¼ to ½ inch of oil in a heavy skillet until very hot—the surface should look wavy.

Using a large serving spoon or a ⅓-cup measure, drop the batter into the oil and cook on both sides until golden brown, about 4 to 6 minutes per side. Drain on the prepared baking sheet and keep in the warm oven until you finish frying the rest of the fritters.

Yield: about 2 dozen fritters, or 8 to 12 servings

Nessa Rabin, waitress.
Favorite Dish: "What do you mean by *dish?*
(A dirty mind makes the day go faster.)"
Other comments: "I'm working on a pamphlet entitled *Miss Manners does River Run* or *This is a Business—We Don't Owe You Anything.*"
Other-other comments: "I love this job. Thank you."

OKRA FRITTERS

These have surprised a lot of people who thought they didn't like okra, and have made a lot of confirmed okra lovers happy.

3 eggs, beaten
1 cup buttermilk or whole milk
1½ cups all-purpose flour
1 cup yellow cornmeal
2 teaspoons salt
2 teaspoons freshly ground black pepper
½ teaspoon dried thyme
½ teaspoon cayenne pepper (optional, but good)
1 pound fresh or frozen okra, cut into ½-inch-thick rounds (stem ends
    trimmed and discarded)
½ medium onion, peeled and chopped (about ½ cup)
½ medium green bell pepper, seeded and chopped (about ½ cup)
1 small stalk celery, trimmed and chopped (about ½ cup)
Canola oil, for frying (⅔ to 1½ cups for a 10-inch skillet)
Ketchup, hot pepper vinegar, or River Run Breakfastlunchanddinner
    Garlic Sauce (source on page xx), for serving

In a large bowl, mix together the eggs and buttermilk (or whole milk). Add the flour, cornmeal, salt, black pepper, thyme, and cayenne (if using) and mix well. Add the okra, onion, bell pepper, and celery and stir until well blended. Let sit at room temperature for 10 to 15 minutes.

Laura Paris, part of the River Run
family from day one.

Set the oven to warm. Line a baking sheet with a brown paper bag or paper towels.

Heat ¼ to ½ inch of oil in a heavy skillet until very hot—the surface should look wavy.

When the oil is ready, gently drop the batter into the oil by large spoonfuls (to make 3-inch fritters) and fry until golden brown, turning to cook the other side. (Each side will take 4 or 5 minutes.) Don't crowd the pan, or it will be difficult to flip the cakes. When done, remove the fritters with a slotted spoon and drain on the prepared baking sheet. Set in the oven to keep warm while you fry the remaining fritters.

Serve as soon as possible with your topping of choice.

Yield: about sixteen 3-inch fritters, or 8 servings

GRIT CAKES

Think of Grit Cakes as the bread for a sandwich or the crust for a pizza. The possibilities are endless. We use them as a base for Huevos Rancheros (page 177). We also serve them with Crawfish Creole Sauce (page 175) and BBQ Sauce (page 196). Other tasty toppings include Hot Pepper Hollandaise (page 171), Dill Gravy (page 189), Cheese Sauce (page 173), or just plain, pure, Vermont maple syrup.

> 6 cups water
> 2 teaspoons salt, plus more to taste
> 4 cups regular (not instant) grits
> 1 cup half-and-half
> 2 eggs, lightly beaten
> 1 cup buttermilk
> 1 to 1½ cups all-purpose flour
> Freshly ground black pepper, to taste
> Canola oil, for frying (⅔ to 1½ cups for a 10-inch skillet)

In a heavy-bottomed pot or Dutch oven, bring the water to a boil. Add the two teaspoons of salt. Stir in the grits, ½ cup at a time; they will thicken up almost immediately. Remove from the heat, add the half-and-half, and stir well. Set aside to cool a bit. Then add the beaten eggs, stirring briskly to mix them in.

Spoon the grits into a greased 13-by-9-inch pan and smooth the top with a spatula or table knife so that the mixture is spread evenly. Allow to cool.

Cover with plastic wrap and refrigerate the grits until thoroughly set up; a few hours will work, but overnight is best.

When ready to cook, remove the grits from the fridge and run a table knife around the edge. Invert onto a flat surface and cut into 12 squares, triangles, diamonds, or whatever shape suits you.

Pour the buttermilk into a shallow bowl and put the flour in a second shallow bowl. Season the flour with salt and pepper.

Set the oven to warm. Line a baking sheet with a brown paper bag or paper towels.

Heat ¼ to ½ inch of oil in a heavy skillet until very hot—the surface should look wavy.

Dip each grit cake in the buttermilk (be sure to cover all sides) and then dredge in the seasoned flour (all sides). Fry for about 5 to 7 minutes on one side, until quite golden. Turn and fry until the second side is getting brown, maybe 5 minutes. Don't crowd the skillet, or it will be it hard to turn the cakes. Drain on the prepared baking sheet and keep warm in the oven until you finish frying all the cakes.

Alternatively, you can broil or grill the grit cakes. Skip the buttermilk and seasoned flour. Instead, brush each side lightly with oil; broil or grill until brown and crispy.

Serve warm with the topping of your choice.

Yield: 12 grit cakes, or 6 servings

BLACK-EYED PEA CAKES

We created many of our fritters, cakes, soups, and omelets from leftovers. That's how the black-eyed peas left over from a Thursday night dinner became black-eyed pea cakes. They were so popular served the next day with eggs and toast that they are now the number-one reason we cook black-eyed peas.

1 pound dried black-eyed peas (to make about 6 cups, cooked)

1¼ cups all-purpose flour

1 cup yellow cornmeal

2 eggs, beaten

½ medium onion, peeled and chopped (about ½ cup)

¼ medium green bell pepper, seeded and chopped (about ¼ cup)

¼ medium red bell pepper, seeded and chopped (about ¼ cup)

½ small stalk celery, trimmed and chopped (about ¼ cup)

1 or 2 jalapeño peppers, stemmed, seeded, and chopped (optional, but good)

1 tablespoon minced garlic

½ teaspoon dried thyme

½ teaspoon dried basil

½ teaspoon white pepper

Salt, to taste

Freshly ground black pepper, to taste

Canola oil, for frying (about ⅔ cup for a 10-inch skillet)

Ranchero Sauce (page 177), Dill Gravy (page 189), or tomato salsa of your choice, for serving

The night before you are going to cook the pea cakes, rinse the peas and pick them over, discarding any small stones or funny-looking peas. Soak the peas overnight in enough cold water to cover by several inches.

Taylore Grymonnt, doctor of oriental medicine.

The next morning, drain the peas. Return them to the pot, cover them with several inches of water again, and bring the pot to a boil. Reduce to a simmer and cook until the peas are tender (this usually takes about an hour, but the time depends on the age of the peas). Drain the peas and set them aside.

If you have forgotten to soak the peas overnight or don't have the time, use the quick-soak method: Prepare the peas as above, but instead of soaking them overnight, bring them to a boil. Boil for 2 minutes, shut off the heat, and let the peas sit for about an hour. Drain them and proceed to cook as above.

Mash the cooked peas with a potato masher or the back of a large spoon, just enough to break them up a little bit.

Combine the peas, ¾ cup of the flour, ½ cup of the cornmeal, and all the remaining ingredients (except the oil and topping) in a large bowl and mix well. With your hands, form the mixture into 3-inch cakes. (This part is messy.)

Mix the remaining ½ cup flour and ½ cup cornmeal in a shallow bowl. Lightly dust each side of each pea cake in this mixture.

Set the oven to warm. Line a baking sheet with a brown paper bag or paper towels.

Heat about ¼ inch of oil in heavy skillet until very hot—the surface should look wavy.

Working in small batches, fry the pea cakes for about 3 to 5 minutes, flipping about halfway through. Don't crowd the pan, or it will be difficult to flip the cakes. Drain on the prepared baking sheet and keep warm in the oven until you finish frying the rest of the cakes.

Serve with the desired topping.

Yield: about 18 cakes, or 6 to 9 servings

MAPLE SYRUP (A.K.A. "VERMONT GOLD")

In the late winter and early spring, legions of Vermonters can be seen slogging through the mud and dirty snow with one purpose in mind: sugaring (that's Vermontese for "making maple syrup"). Thousands of maple trees are tapped and their sap collected, boiled down to syrup, and packed—all in a frenzied few weeks. If you ever visit a sugarhouse in March—steam billowing out the cupola, the sugarmaker busy stoking the evaporator—you'll appreciate the hard work involved and understand why the product costs what it does. Keep in mind that it takes about 40 gallons of sap to make 1 gallon of syrup.

At River Run we buy syrup from Bill Smith, whose family has been sugaring on Maple Ridge Farm in Plainfield since the forties. Bill runs a large-scale operation, producing 500 to 700 gallons of syrup a year with his wood-fired

Bill Smith, farmer.

evaporator. He sells most of it locally and some by mail order. During sugaring season, he says, visitors are always welcome at the sugarhouse.

And it's hard to beat a sugarhouse in spring. It's the perfect refuge from mud season, Vermont's infamous "fifth season," which occurs when all the freezing and thawing that makes the sap run also turns the state's 7,000-plus miles of dirt roads into deep, vehicle-gobbling mud. (See "Mud Season Poem.") It's warm inside a sugarhouse, and the steam smells slightly sweet. There's enough work going on to give everyone a sense of purpose, but enough time left for visiting. If you're lucky, someone may stop by with homemade raised doughnuts, the traditional sugarhouse snack.

After the sap is boiled, it is graded by color: the lighter the syrup, the more delicate the flavor and the higher the grade—and the cost. The choice of grade is a matter for your taste buds and wallet to decide, as well as what use you plan to make of the syrup. You may want a lighter syrup to pour on your pancakes but a darker syrup for cooking and baking.

Somewhat confusing is the fact that the U.S.D.A. has instituted one grading system, and Vermont, which prides itself on quality control, has another.

From lightest to darkest, the U.S. system goes like this: U.S. Grade A Light Amber, U.S. Grade A Medium Amber, U.S. Grade A Dark Amber, U.S. Grade B.

Vermont uses the following grades: Vermont Fancy, Vermont Grade A Medium Amber, Vermont Grade A Dark Amber, Vermont Grade B.

But you don't have to worry too much about it.

It's all good.

Note: Once it is opened, store maple syrup in the refrigerator or, better yet, in the freezer. It won't freeze solid but will keep perfectly for months.

To order Bill Smith's syrup, write to Maple Ridge Farm, 626 Taylor Farm Road, Plainfield, VT 05667.

MUD SEASON POEM

In the spring
Vermont birds sing
And to our luck
It's full of muck
And you might get stuck
In the gluck
Unless you have a 4WD truck.

Excerpted from "A Poem About the Seasons" (1991), by Billy Spence, grade 6, Calais Elementary School, Calais, Vermont. Printed with permission of the author.

Whenever Jackson Teague visits River Run from Brooklyn,
he requests "the usual"—heart-shaped pancakes.

FAMOUS BUTTERMILK PANCAKES

These pancakes were famously popular with our customers way before the *New York Times* wrote them up ("terrific pancakes, thick and puffy, but dense and crisp around the edges," Sunday Travel section, 9/21/97). One of our secrets is whipping the egg whites. Another is serving the pancakes with pure maple syrup from Bill Smith's sugarhouse, just up the road.

3 cups all-purpose flour

3 tablespoons light brown sugar

1½ teaspoons baking powder

1½ teaspoons baking soda

½ teaspoon salt

3 eggs

3 cups buttermilk

8 tablespoons (1 stick) unsalted butter, melted and allowed to cool slightly

Solid vegetable shortening or vegetable oil, for greasing pan

Fruit of choice: blueberries, sliced peaches, sliced strawberries, sliced bananas, etc. (optional)

Warm maple syrup, for serving

Ground cinnamon, allspice, and/or nutmeg, for sprinkling (optional)

Put the flour, brown sugar, baking powder, baking soda, and salt into a large bowl. Stir with a whisk to mix and to break up any lumps in the brown sugar.

Separate the eggs; add the yolks to the flour mixture and refrigerate the whites until ready to use (cold egg whites will whip better).

Add the buttermilk to the flour mixture, whisking to combine. Add the melted, slightly cooled butter and whisk gently some more. (If the butter is too cold, it will congeal; if too hot, it will cook the eggs.) The batter should be fairly smooth.

Whip the chilled egg whites until very, very stiff and scrape them on top of the batter. Using a poking motion with your whisk, incorporate the whites into the batter. They should not be totally mixed in; you should still be able to see a bit of egg white here and there. The batter will be thick and gluey.

Heat a griddle or cast-iron skillet over medium-high heat. Add 1 or 2 teaspoons shortening (don't use butter—it will burn) and swirl to coat the bottom. Test for proper heat by sprinkling a few drops of water on the heated surface; the water will form little sizzling, dancing beads when the skillet is ready.

Spoon a generous cup of batter onto the skillet to form a pancake about 6 inches in diameter. Cook until the bottom is browned and bubbles start to form on top (about 3 to 4 minutes). If you want to make fruit pancakes, add some sliced fruit at this point, just before you flip it over. (If you put the fruit right into the batter, the juices will make it too runny, and it will be difficult to cook the pancakes through.) Flip and cook the other side until browned (3 to 4 minutes more). The pancake should be cooked through.

Continue until the batter is used up, keeping an eye on the heat and adjusting the temperature as necessary. Grease the pan as needed.

Serve plain, with warm maple syrup, with fruit on top, and/or sprinkled with spices.

Yield: 6 or 7 very large (6- to 8-inch) pancakes, about 3 servings

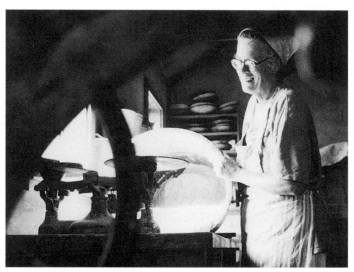

Jules and Helen Rabin.

FRENCH TOAST

At River Run we are fortunate to be able to buy what many people think is some of the best sourdough French bread in the world. It's made by Jules and Helen Rabin in their home-built beehive oven at the nearby Upland Bakers. Whatever bread you choose to use for your French toast—be it your own, from a local bakery, or from the grocery store—you will find this recipe simple and satisfying.

      1 loaf French bread or white bread
      6 eggs
      2 cups half-and-half
      4 tablespoons (really!) vanilla extract
      Several tablespoons unsalted butter, for frying
      Warm maple syrup, for serving

Cut the bread into 1½-inch-thick slices.

Mix the eggs, half-and-half, and vanilla in a medium-sized bowl. Soak the bread in the batter until well saturated (if you use cheap supermarket bread, this will take less than a minute. If you use good-quality, denser bread, it will take a few minutes).

Melt 1 or 2 tablespoons butter in a skillet until it starts to bubble, but don't let it start to brown. Place the soaked bread in the skillet and cook on each side for 4 to 5 minutes, until nice and brown.

Serve immediately with warm maple syrup.

Yield: enough batter for a 22-inch loaf of French bread cut into 14 slices

EASY WHITE BREAD

If you've never baked bread before, this is the recipe to start with. Steve Owens, a musician and teacher who lives in a neighboring town, gave us this recipe, which is simple and produces a delicious spongy loaf. Steve is also known as the creator of a recipe for "blue soup," a cream-based black bean soup that he says tasted "perfectly delicious" but was such an eerie color that neither he nor his wife could eat it, "even in the dark."

Step 1:
2½ cups milk
2 tablespoons maple syrup
1½ tablespoons (two ¼-ounce packets) active dry yeast
3 cups all-purpose flour

Step 2:
2 tablespoons unsalted butter, melted
2 teaspoons salt
3 cups all-purpose flour
Vegetable oil, for coating bowl

Step 1: Scald the milk (heat it to just below boiling) and stir in the maple syrup. Allow the mixture to cool until it is just warm but not hot (put the pot in a snowbank, if one is handy). Transfer to a large mixing bowl, add the yeast, and let it bubble for about 10 minutes. Add the 3 cups of flour, mix, and let sit for 10 or 15 minutes.

Step 2: Add the melted butter, salt, and remaining 3 cups flour to the mixture you created in Step 1, mixing with a spoon or your hands as needed (a big professional-type mixer works with a dough hook works well too). Turn the dough out onto a floured surface and knead a little bit—3 or 4 minutes is fine, and longer is fine too. Scrape out the bowl, coat it with a little oil, and put the dough back in. Cover with a clean dish towel or plastic wrap and allow the dough to rise until doubled in bulk. This will take perhaps an hour in a warm spot, but for an even better texture, stash the covered bowl in the refrigerator for 3 or 4 hours.

Punch the dough down, knead it for about a minute, divide it in half, and place in 2 greased 9-by-5-inch loaf pans. Cover with clean dish towels and let rise another 30 minutes.

Meanwhile, set the oven to 350 degrees. Bake the bread 35 to 40 minutes, or until loaves are golden and the bread sounds hollow when you tap on it.

Yield: 2 loaves

Paula Emery, teacher.

Kenneth
McGeehee.

ORANGE BREAD

We borrowed this recipe—which results in an incredibly moist, sweet loaf—from our good friend Kenneth McGeehee. Jimmy and Kenneth were friends growing up in Mississippi, and fortunately for Jimmy, Kenneth was already living in New York City when Jimmy moved there. Kenneth ran his own catering company in New York and now runs the kitchen at Elizabeth Point Lodge in Fernandina Beach, Florida. We've learned a lot from Kenneth over the years, not only about cooking but also about planning for and presenting a meal, whether it's a large, fancy dinner party or just supper for friends.

½ cup (1 stick) unsalted butter,
   at room temperature
1½ cups sugar
2 eggs
1½ cups all-purpose flour
1 teaspoon baking powder

¼ teaspoon salt
6 tablespoons orange juice
¼ cup whole milk
½ teaspoon grated orange zest
⅓ cup confectioner's sugar

Set the oven to 325 degrees. Grease a 9-by-5-inch loaf pan and set it aside.

In a large mixing bowl, cream the butter with the sugar. Add the eggs and mix well. Set aside.

In a smaller bowl, mix together the flour, baking powder, and salt.

In another small bowl, mix 4 tablespoons (¼ cup) of the o.j. with the milk and orange zest.

Alternate adding the dry ingredients and wet ingredients to the butter mixture. Mix well between additions.

Spoon the batter into the prepared pan. Bake for about 45 minutes, until a tester inserted in the center comes out clean.

Remove from the oven and allow to cool a bit before removing the loaf from the pan. Allow the loaf to cool on a cake rack.

While the bread is still a little warm, make the glaze: Mix the remaining 2 tablespoons orange juice with the confectioner's sugar and, using a spoon, drizzle it over the warm bread.

Yield: 1 loaf, or 4 to 6 servings

Plainfield Volunteer Fire Department.

DAVID MAMET'S BURNT TOAST

Bread
Butter
Coffee or tea, for serving

Burn toast.
Apologize to and dismiss firemen.
Scrape and butter toast. Enjoy with coffee or tea.

CORN BREAD

Jimmy's mom, Carolyn Kennedy Bowen, made corn bread at least four or five times a week for dinner when he was growing up. His dad loved it; he used to crumble up the leftovers into a big ol' glass of buttermilk, add a little salt and pepper, and eat it with a spoon.

3 cups yellow cornmeal
3 cups all-purpose flour
¾ cups sugar, plus more for sprinkling (optional)
2¼ teaspoons salt
3 tablespoons baking powder
1¼ cups vegetable oil
3 eggs
3 cups milk

Set oven to 450 degrees.

In a very large bowl, mix together the cornmeal, flour, sugar (if using), salt, and baking powder. Set aside.

Pour the oil into a 10-inch cast-iron skillet and place it in the preheated oven until it bubbles, 5 to 10 minutes.

While the oil is heating, mix together the eggs and milk in a small bowl, beating well with a fork. Pour the wet ingredients into the dry ingredients and mix, then stir in the very hot oil, a bit at a time. It will not incorporate into the batter perfectly, but that's OK. The idea here is to give the batter a jump-start on cooking.

Pour the batter into the hot skillet (you don't need to grease it; the residual oil will do the job). Sprinkle a bit of sugar on top for taste and looks. Bake until brown or until your tester comes out clean, about 25 minutes.

Allow the corn bread to sit in the pan for an hour so it can be easily removed. Serve ASAP.

Yield: one 10-inch round loaf

Nancy Huelsberg with her grandchildren, Lucy and Caleb Basa.

NADINE'S ONION & BLACK PEPPER ROLLS

Nadine's is a neighborhood restaurant in New York's Greenwich Village; Jimmy was a partner in the business for many years. These rolls are served at Nadine's as soon as a customer sits down at a table. They've been written up in *Gourmet* magazine and various newspapers.

1½ cups warm water
1 scant tablespoon (one ¼-ounce packet) active dry yeast
6 tablespoons vegetable oil
2½ cups chopped onions (about 2½ medium)
5 cups all-purpose flour
2 teaspoons salt
1 tablespoon coarsely ground black pepper
1½ teaspoons poppy seeds

Pour the warm water into a small bowl and sprinkle the yeast on top. Let sit for 5 to 10 minutes; the yeast should start to bubble.

Meanwhile, heat 2 tablespoons of the oil in a skillet set over medium-high heat. Add the onions, reduce the heat to medium, and sauté them until they are quite soft, 10 to 12 minutes. Set aside to cool a bit.

In a large bowl, mix the flour, salt, pepper, and poppy seeds.

Add the yeast mixture and the remaining 4 tablespoons (¼ cup) oil. Add the cooked onions. Stir vigorously. A big professional–type mixer with a dough hook works well too.

Turn the dough out onto a floured surface and knead until smooth, at least 4 or 5 minutes.

Clean out the mixing bowl, grease it with a bit of oil, and put the kneaded dough back in. Cover it with a clean dish towel or plastic wrap and let rise in a warm place for 1 hour. The dough should be doubled in size, and when you press it with your fingers, it should stay indented. (If it doesn't, let it rise some more.)

Put the dough on a floured surface and knead it a minute or two. Cut it into quarters, and cut each quarter into 3 pieces, to make 1 dozen rolls. With your hands, form each piece into an oval.

Place on greased baking sheets, cover with clean dish towels, and let rise in a warm spot for 30 minutes.

Set the oven to 400 degrees.

Bake the rolls for about 20 minutes, or until golden.

Yield: 12 rolls

Denise Wands, carpenter: "Let's start off with the coffee. Best java in the USA. I like to start my weekend mornings with BBQ catfish, fried green tomatoes, and a buttermilk biscuit. You just can't find home-cooked food like the River Run's anywhere. Thank you, Jimmy and Maya."

REALLY BIG BUTTERMILK BISCUITS

Our biscuits are the foundation of "B & G" (Biscuits and Gravy) and Dixie Eggs (page 188). But many of our customers order biscuits in place of toast, or just by themselves. Not only are they really big, but they are really delicious.

5 cups all-purpose flour
2½ teaspoons baking powder
1¼ teaspoons baking soda
1 teaspoon salt

12 tablespoons (1½ sticks)
   unsalted butter, well chilled
2½ cups buttermilk

Set the oven to 450 degrees. Grease a baking sheet or line it with baking parchment.

In a large bowl, stir together the flour, baking powder, baking soda, and salt. Cut the butter into small pieces and distribute throughout the flour. Then, using a pastry blender or your fingers, mash the butter into the flour until the mixture is the consistency of coarse cornmeal. (You can also do this with a food processor.)

Add the buttermilk and mix briefly, just until all the dry ingredients are incorporated into the dough. Overmixing will make the biscuits tough.

Turn the dough out onto a very well-floured surface and knead it briefly, working in a bit more flour so that it is not totally sticky. Pat it out to a thickness of 1½ to 2 inches. Cut with a 3½-inch round cookie cutter or the floured rim of a large drinking glass.

Place the first biscuit at the center the prepared baking sheet. Nestle the other biscuits around the first one so the sides are touching. Bake 15 to 20 minutes, or until golden brown.

Remove from oven and allow to cool somewhat. Break them apart into individual biscuits and serve warm.

Yield: 8 or 9 really big biscuits

CINNAMON BUNS

These are a quick and easy (and equally delicious) alternative to traditional cinnamon buns (the kind made with a yeast dough). When it comes to the amount of filling you need to use, we follow the directions of our former baker, Nicole Graves, to use a "free-for-all" of ingredients.

For the buns:
1 recipe biscuit dough (page 64), made with the addition of ½ cup
     sugar
8 tablespoons (1 stick) unsalted butter
Any or all of the following, to taste:
   Granulated sugar
   Light brown sugar
   Ground cinnamon
   Ground nutmeg
   Chopped nuts (walnuts, pecans, and/or hazelnuts)
   Raisins (dark and/or golden)

For the icing (optional):
½ cup confectioner's sugar
2 teaspoons water
Few drops vanilla extract

Set the oven to 450 degrees. Grease 2 baking sheets and set aside.

On a well-floured board, pat out the biscuit dough to about ⅜ inch thick. Cut butter into small pieces and distribute over the dough. Liberally sprinkle sugar and cinnamon over the dough and any or all of the other ingredients that you like, making sure to sprinkle them evenly and not to neglect the edges of the dough.

Roll up the dough tightly, as you would a jelly roll. Fold over the ends so the filling doesn't fall out. With a very sharp knife, cut the dough into slices about an inch thick or thicker, as you wish.

Place on the prepared baking sheets, giving each piece room to spread a bit, and bake 15 to 20 minutes, or until golden brown. Remove the buns from the baking sheets and allow to cool slightly on cake racks.

Make the icing (if using): Combine the confectioner's sugar with the water and vanilla. Using a spoon, drizzle over the top of the warm buns.

Best served warm.

Yield: about 12 cinnamon buns

Sierra Lowell.

APRICOT SCONES

These scones are very creamy and pleasantly tart. Serve warm with pure Vermont honey on the side.

3½ cups all-purpose flour
½ cup sugar
2 tablespoons baking powder
½ teaspoon baking soda
½ teaspoon salt
12 tablespoons (1½ sticks) cold unsalted butter

2 eggs, beaten
1 cup buttermilk
3 to 4 fresh apricots, pitted and diced to make 1 cup, or 1 cup chopped dried apricots
1 tablespoon sugar, for sprinkling

Set the oven to 400 degrees. Line a baking sheet with baking parchment and set it aside.

Sift the flour, sugar, baking powder, baking soda, and salt into a large mixing bowl. Cut the butter into chunks. Using 2 knives, a pastry blender, or your fingers, work in the cold butter until the mixture is coarse but the butter lumps are still visible.

In another bowl, mix the eggs and buttermilk and add to the dry ingredients. Mix lightly. Add the apricots and mix.

Pat the dough out on a floured surface to a thickness of about ¾-inch. Use a 3-inch cookie cutter or the floured rim of a drinking glass to cut out scones, or cut the dough into diamond shapes. Place on the prepared baking sheet, about 1½ inches apart. Sprinkle a tablespoon of sugar over all.

Bake about 20 minutes, or until lightly browned.

Yield: about twelve 3-inch round scones

BLUEBERRY COFFEE CAKE

This tastes like a really great blueberry muffin, but unlike most muffins, it is just as good when cooled as it is right-from-the-oven.

For the cake:

2 cups all-purpose flour

2½ teaspoons baking powder

¼ teaspoon salt

4 tablespoons (½ stick) unsalted butter, at room temperature

¾ cup sugar

1 egg

¾ cup milk, preferably whole milk

2 cups fresh or frozen blueberries

For the topping:

½ cup sugar

⅓ cup all-purpose flour

½ teaspoon ground cinnamon

4 tablespoons (½ stick) unsalted butter, at room temperature

For the icing:

½ cup confectioner's sugar

2 teaspoons water

Few drops vanilla extract

Set the oven to 350 degrees. Grease a 9-inch round cake pan and set it aside. In a medium bowl, blend the flour, baking powder, and salt.

In a large mixing bowl, cream the butter with the sugar, then add the egg and mix well. Add the dry ingredients to this bowl and mix. Then add the milk and mix again. Carefully fold in the berries. Pour the batter into the prepared cake pan and set it aside.

Make the topping: In a small bowl, mix the topping ingredients together. Use your fingers to work in the butter until the mixture is crumbly.

Sprinkle the topping over the top of the cake batter and bake 45 to 50 minutes, or until a tester inserted in the middle comes out clean or almost clean. Let cool on a cake rack.

Make the icing: Combine the confectioner's sugar with the water and vanilla. Using a spoon, drizzle it over the top of the warm cake.

Serve the coffee cake from the pan, warm or at room temperature.

Yield: one 9-inch cake, or 6 to 8 servings

Marty Levin.

MARTY'S GRANOLA

Maya's mom, Charlotte, is our neighbor down the road, and Marty Levin, Maya's best friend's mom, is our neighbor up the road. Marty is a great gardener, neighbor, and cook. It is her recipe for this exceptional granola that we use at River Run. It's wonderful for breakfast, but it also works as a trail mix for hiking and camping. Pack it in Mason jars, and it makes welcome Christmas presents too. You may want to make a double batch while you're at it; it keeps well in the freezer up to three months.

4 cups regular (not quick-cooking) rolled oats

2 cups wheat flakes (available in health-food stores)

1 cup sunflower seeds, or to taste

1 cup coarsely chopped almonds, or to taste

¾ cup canola oil

¾ cup dark maple syrup (grade B if available; see page 47)

3 tablespoons water

2 teaspoons vanilla extract

71

Set the oven to 300 degrees. Grease a 17-by–12-inch jelly-roll pan or two 13-by-9-inch brownie pans with a generous amount of canola oil or cooking spray.

In a large bowl, mix together the oats, wheat flakes, sunflower seeds, and almonds.

In a saucepan, warm the oil, syrup, water, and vanilla. The mixture may separate and look spotty (kind of like a lava lamp), but that's OK. Pour the warm mixture over the oat mixture and mix well, using a large spoon or your hands.

Spread the granola in a shallow layer in the prepared pan (or pans). Bake for approximately 45 minutes, stirring well every 15 minutes. As soon as you remove the pan from the oven, scrape the bottom with a metal spatula so the granola doesn't stick. Set the pan on a rack and allow the mixture to cool. The granola will be soft when you take it out of the oven but will crisp up as it cools.

Store in an airtight container up to 2 weeks or freeze up to 3 months.

Yield: about 8 cups

CHAPTER 3
WEEKEND SPECIALS

Some customers come for our biscuits. Some come for our mashed potatoes or fried green tomatoes. But by and large, most of our customers come for the Weekend Specials, a continually changing menu of main dishes that we hope will rouse their interest and appetites.

We started serving Weekend Specials when we first opened, but back then they consisted simply of larger portions of our weekday fare. The portions are still large, but now weekends are the time when the kitchen pulls out all the stops. We might put BBQ Spaghetti (one of our favorites) on the menu, or Chicken-Fried Hamburger Steak, or an omelet filled with shrimp, peppers, and goat cheese, or a jambalaya made with catfish and andouille sausage. We round out the offerings with popular "sides": Fried Green Tomatoes, Okra Fritters, and such. It's a busy and kind of festive time of the week. Many of our customers have their favorites and request them regularly. We are happy to oblige.

Some of the "specials" recipes here are classics with a River Run twist. Some are from our friends and family. Others are pure River Run creations.

Coming up with ideas for "specials" is one of the most enjoyable and rewarding aspects of running a kitchen—whether it's in a restaurant or at home. At River Run every weekend is different, and we are always changing things up, always learning and trying out new ideas. We hope these recipes inspire you to do the same.

OMELETS

We've developed three main rules for making perfect omelets.

The first is to use canola oil, not butter or olive oil (they burn). The second is to get the pan quite hot before putting in the oil, and then to allow the oil to get quite hot before putting in the eggs. The third is to finish the omelet under the broiler, which makes it puff up and form ridges and brown ever so slightly. It is possible to finish an omelet in a hot oven, but often the bottom overcooks or the omelet gets tough.

If you want to fill your omelet with cheese, add it just before you put the skillet under the broiler. Prepare any other fillings ahead of time, and heat them in a separate pan just before making the omelet so they are good and hot when the omelet is done. Plan on using 1 cup of filling per three-egg omelet.

We fill omelets with almost anything: meat, vegetables, poultry, and cheese in many combinations. One of Maya's favorites is the Sunday Dinner Omelet, which uses the leftovers from Sunday dinner: roast beef or chicken or ham, with peas, mashed potatoes, and gravy. We have included a list of some of our favorite combinations, but think of these as just a bunch of suggestions; your own pantry and fridge will provide lots of inspiration.

There is no getting around the fact that omelets are a short-order dish; you should make them and serve them immediately—sitting around does not improve them. So don't try to make them for a crowd. But since they take only a few minutes each, you can easily produce delicious hot omelets for three or four people in a very reasonable amount of time. Just have all your ingredients ready to go.

3 eggs
1 tablespoon water
1 to 2 teaspoons canola oil (to coat bottom of a 6- to 8-inch skillet)
About 1 cup filling of your choice, warm (see suggestions)

Preheat the broiler.

Whisk the eggs together in a bowl. Add the water and whisk some more.

Set a small skillet over medium-high heat for a minute or so. Add the oil and heat, rotating the pan slightly to spread the oil evenly. When quite hot, add the eggs. As soon as the eggs start to set (5 to 10 seconds), begin pushing the edges of the omelet toward the center with a rubber spatula or wooden spoon.

When the bottom of the omelet seems to be set but the top is still quite runny (30 to 45 seconds), put the pan under the broiler, 3 to 4 inches from the heat. (If filling with cheese, sprinkle it on just before you put the omelet under the broiler.) Broil until the eggs are set and puffed, about 1 minute. If the top begins to brown a little bit, that's OK.

Remove the omelet from the pan. Put the warm filling of your choice on one half of the omelet, fold over the other half, and serve immediately.

Yield: 1 serving

Suggested Fillings for Omelets: Be sure to give yourself enough time to assemble, chop, sauté, and heat these ingredients, as necessary, before you start cooking the eggs.

- Cooked sausage, sage, chopped green onions, and grated cheddar
- Pulled Pork (page 134), sautéed onions, and cheddar
- Wilted spinach, caramelized onions, and feta cheese

- Sautéed andouille sausage, sautéed bell peppers and onions, and grated cheddar
- Sautéed sausage and onions, home fries, and grated cheddar
- Roast beef or baked ham, mashed potatoes, peas, and gravy
- Ham, fried okra, and grated cheddar
- Sun-dried tomatoes, wilted spinach, and grated mozzarella
- Grilled shrimp, roasted red pepper, and chèvre
- Roasted red pepper, roasted garlic, sautéed mushrooms, and sour cream
- Sautéed mushrooms, chopped green onions, and Brie
- Steamed asparagus, sautéed mushrooms, and blue cheese
- Chopped tomato, fresh basil, and feta cheese
- Ham, black-eyed peas, and grated cheddar
- Sautéed apples or pears and blue cheese
- Cooked chicken, corn, tomatillos, chopped red onion, and grated Monterey Jack
- Fresh basil, thyme, parsley, chopped tomato, and feta cheese
- Sliced grilled hot dogs, chopped onions, and American cheese
- Chopped Meat Loaf (page 101) and grated cheddar
- Corn, tomato, sautéed onions, mashed potatoes, and Dill Gravy (page 189)
- Cooked sausage, jalapeños, sautéed shallots and mushrooms, and grated mozzarella
- Bacon, crumbled cooked hamburger, sautéed onions, chopped tomato, and blue cheese
- Steamed green beans, sautéed garlic, and cream cheese
- Anchovies cooked with capers, tomato, garlic, and spinach
- Fried okra, chopped tomatoes, and grated cheddar

Lylehaven Farm: Sue Brown, and farmworkers. Lylehaven is a first-class Holstein breeding and dairy farm. Jimmy's buddy Jayson worked there for a while and is probably responsible for bringing the crew to River Run. They are now some of our most popular and regular customers.

- Cooked shrimp, red bell pepper, and Hot Pepper Hollandaise (page 171)
- Bacon, sautéed mushrooms, and blue cheese
- Mashed sweet potatoes, caramelized apples, and red onion
- Steamed green beans, pesto, and tomato sauce
- Chopped fresh chilies and grated cheddar
- BBQ Chicken (page 137), sautéed onions, and grated cheddar
- Sausage, sautéed apples, and grated cheddar
- Sautéed portobello, shiitake, and/or oyster mushrooms and grated Parmesan

78

VEGGIE SCRAMBLER

Eggs, vegetables and cheese: simple enough, but almost every table in the restaurant, from 6 in the morning until 3 in the afternoon, orders at least one Veggie Scrambler. Jimmy and "the boys" (as the kitchen staffers refer to themselves) like to add a little bacon or sausage to theirs. Serve for breakfast with home fries and toast, for lunch with Jo-Jos (page 157) or French fries, and for dinner with a baked potato.

> 2 to 3 teaspoons canola oil
> 4 to 6 cups mixed chopped vegetables (suggestions include onions, mushrooms, carrots, yellow squash, zucchini, cabbage, broccoli, cauliflower, green beans, and bell peppers)
> 1 to 2 tablespoons water
> 4 to 6 eggs, beaten
> 1 cup grated cheddar

Heat 2 teaspoons of the oil in a skillet set over medium-high heat. When it starts to sizzle, add the vegetables and cook for a minute or two, flipping and stirring them. Now add the water; you don't want to drown the vegetables, you just want to steam them. Cover the pan with a lid and let cook for a few minutes. Every once in a while, remove the lid and give the vegetables a good flip or stir. Cook until they are tender but still crisp. If any water is left in the pan, drain it off. Take the pan off the heat and leave it, covered, until ready to use.

Heat another skillet, preferably one of the non-stick variety, over medium heat. If you are not using a non-stick pan, add another teaspoon or so of oil.

When the pan is hot, add the eggs and scramble until almost done to your liking. Add the vegetables and stir, cooking a bit more. Add the cheese and stir, cooking until it is melted.

Yield: 2 servings

PATRICK'S FANCY HOMES

Patrick was one of our first customers, and one day he asked if we could make a simple plate of home fries with lots of vegetables and cheese melted on top. When his plate came out, everyone wanted to know what Patrick was having. Ever since, Patrick's Fancy Homes has been one of our most popular dishes.

4 large or 6 medium baking potatoes, scrubbed but not peeled

6 to 8 cups chopped vegetables, chopped separately (we usually use a combination of onions, mushrooms, carrots, yellow squash, zucchini, cabbage, broccoli, cauliflower, green beans, green and/or red bell peppers, and peeled eggplant)

4 tablespoons canola oil

1 teaspoon salt

1 teaspoon freshly ground black pepper

1 teaspoon garlic powder

2 to 3 tablespoons water

2 cups grated sharp cheddar cheese, or more to taste

Patrick Giantonio is a human rights activist and a baker. He currently works with Vermont Refugee Assistance and is the owner of Patrick's Green Mountain Twisters (a pretzel company).

Cut potatoes into 1- or 1½- inch cubes. Place them in a large pot and cover them with cold water. Bring the water to a boil. Continue boiling until a fork will pierce the potatoes easily. Drain.

Meanwhile, cut the vegetables into somewhat uniform, bite-sized pieces.

Heat 3 tablespoons of the oil on a griddle or in a skillet. When the oil is hot, add the cooked potatoes and flip with a spatula or metal spoon. Add the salt, pepper, and garlic powder and continue to flip the potatoes and scrape the griddle with the spatula. When potatoes are almost browned to your liking, begin sautéing the vegetables.

Heat the remaining tablespoon of oil in another skillet. When hot, add the vegetables, starting with the ones that take the longest to cook, such as eggplant, carrots, onions, cauliflower, and broccoli. Then add the ones that take the least time to cook, like mushrooms, bell peppers, and summer squash. Now add the water; you don't want to drown the vegetables, just steam them. Cover the pan with a lid and let cook for a few minutes. Every once in a while, remove the lid and give the vegetables a good flip or stir. Cook until they are tender but still crisp. If any water is left in the pan, drain it off.

Preheat the broiler.

When vegetables are tender, place the home fries on a flameproof platter or casserole dish. Place the vegetables on the homes and top with the cheese. Place the dish under the broiler, about 4 inches from the heat, until the cheese is melted.

Yield: about 4 servings

SCRAPPLE

Jimmy didn't grow up eating scrapple—it's something he discovered and began enjoying for breakfast during his stint as a legislative assistant in Washington, D.C., in the early 1980s. On weekend trips to Bethany Beach, Delaware, he and his friends would stop at Skeeter's, a small breakfast-and-lunch place not unlike River Run, except it served beer at breakfast. They'd eat scrapple and shoot a couple games of pool before heading off to the beach.

1 pound ground pork or loose mild pork sausage
5 cups beef or chicken stock or canned broth
2 cups yellow cornmeal, preferably coarse-ground
2 teaspoons salt
2 teaspoons garlic powder
1 teaspoon freshly ground black pepper
½ to 1 teaspoon cayenne pepper
1 teaspoon white pepper
1 teaspoon ground cumin

In a large skillet, brown the ground pork (or sausage) over medium heat, stirring frequently. While the pork is browning, heat the broth in a large heavy saucepan or Dutch oven until it is almost boiling.

When the meat is completely browned, remove it from the skillet with a slotted spoon and add it to the hot broth. Bring the broth and pork to a boil, reduce the heat to medium-low, and add the cornmeal a little at a time, stirring constantly to prevent lumps (a few won't hurt). When all the cornmeal

Darlene Carey, special educator and caterer, and her dad, Richard Carey, food service purveyor. "It's like having a seat in Grandma's kitchen."

has been added, continue cooking and stirring until the mixture thickens, 5 to 7 minutes. Remove from the heat and stir in the seasonings. Place the mixture in a lightly greased 9-by-5-inch loaf pan. Allow to cool to room temperature, cover with plastic wrap, and refrigerate for several hours or overnight. (You can make the scrapple up to this point 1 or 2 days ahead.)

When the scrapple is thoroughly cooled, remove it from the loaf pan by turning it upside down on a cutting board. Slice the scrapple loaf with a sharp knife into ½-inch or ¾-inch-thick slices. Grease a skillet lightly and heat over medium-high heat. Cook the scrapple slices until browned on both sides, 3 to 5 minutes on each side. Drain on paper towels and serve with eggs, home fries, and toast.

Yield: 10 to 12 slices, or 5 to 6 servings

BREAKFAST PASTA

This dish is very similar to pasta alla carbonara, except we throw in ham and sausage with the bacon and serve it for breakfast. It's a great use for plain leftover pasta; you can adjust the ingredients according to how much pasta you have on hand.

6 eggs, beaten
¾ cup freshly grated Parmesan cheese
½ teaspoon salt
½ teaspoon freshly ground black pepper
1 tablespoon minced fresh parsley
1 to 1½ pounds chopped bacon, sausage, and/or ham
2 teaspoons olive oil
1 pound pasta (cooked)

Mix the eggs, ½ cup of the Parmesan, and the salt, pepper, and parsley in a bowl with a fork or whisk.

Line a plate with paper towels.

In a skillet, cook whatever meats you are using. The bacon should be fairly crisp, the sausage cooked through, and the ham browned. Remove from the skillet with a slotted spoon and set aside to drain on the lined plate.

Heat the oil in a large skillet over medium-high heat. Throw in the pasta and flip or stir for a minute or two. Add the egg mixture and stir while cooking for another minute or two. The eggs will coat the pasta and set right away.

Add the meat and cook for another couple of minutes, just until everything is good and hot.

Plate and sprinkle the remaining ¼ cup Parmesan on the pasta. Serve immediately.

Yield: 3 to 4 servings

Jerry and Kathy Kilcourse, former
hardware-store owners.

BBQ SPAGHETTI

Fishermen have their "go-to" lure—reliable in a pinch—and cooks have a "go-to" dish. This is ours, not only at the restaurant but also at home. Breakfast, lunch, or dinner.

½ pound meat, poultry, fish, or vegetables, leftover or fresh (optional)
1 cup BBQ Sauce, to taste (page 196)
2 teaspoons canola oil
½ medium onion, peeled and chopped (about ½ cup)
½ pound fresh spinach, stemmed and rinsed
½ pound spaghetti or other pasta, cooked (leftovers are great)

If using leftover meat, poultry, fish, or vegetables, heat them through in a skillet or microwave. If they are not yet cooked, cook them to your liking.

Heat the BBQ sauce in a small saucepan set over low heat.

Meanwhile, heat the oil in a large covered skillet or pot with a lid and sauté the onion until it starts to brown, 10 to 12 minutes. Toss in the spinach, cover, and cook 2 minutes.

Add the cooked pasta and ¼ to ½ cup of the BBQ sauce; continue cooking until the pasta is heated through and the spinach has wilted.

Plate the pasta and place the cooked meat, poultry, chicken, fish, or vegetables (if using) right on top. (We prefer not to slice the meat or chicken.) Spoon or pour as much warm BBQ sauce over the top as you like.

Serve immediately.

Yield: 2 servings

PIZZETTAS

Grilled little pizzas, pizzettas make great appetizers or side dishes for a cookout. If you want, make the dough a day ahead of time and grill it, then refrigerate the pizzettas for the next day, when you can top and broil them.

1 cup warm water
1 tablespoon honey
1 scant tablespoon (one ¼-ounce packet) active dry yeast
3 cups all-purpose flour
1 teaspoon salt
1 tablespoon olive oil
Toppings of choice: We suggest our Pizza Sauce (page 183) and mozzarella; andouille sausage, tomato sauce, caramelized onions, and grated cheddar; or basil, fresh tomatoes, and crumbled feta.

In a small bowl, mix the warm water and honey. Sprinkle the yeast on top and let sit for 5 to 10 minutes. The mixture should start to bubble.

In a separate, larger bowl, mix the flour and salt. Add the yeast mixture and olive oil. Mix well with your hands, kneading the dough in the bowl until all the dry ingredients are incorporated. Cover the bowl with plastic wrap and let rise for about two hours, until the dough has doubled in bulk.

Grease the grill rack using a pastry brush dipped in oil or spraying with cooking spray. Prepare a fire for grilling. Preheat the broiler as well.

To make the pizzettas, punch the dough down and knead it a little in the bowl. Pinch off a piece of dough and form it into a ball a little bigger than a golf ball. Roll it out on a well-floured surface until very thin—it should be

88

about 6 or 7 inches in diameter—and place on the grill for a few minutes on each side, just until it starts to brown. It will cook more when you finish it under the broiler.

Remove from the grill, add your choice of toppings, and broil 3 to 4 inches from the heat until the cheese melts and/or the toppings are sizzling.

Yield: about 8 individual pizzas, 6 to 7 inches in diameter (8 servings)

Leda Schubert, writer and school library
consultant; Bob Rosenfeld, mathematician
and statistician; and Winnie.

VEGGIE BURGERS

Light and flavorful, these came to us from Josh Grinker. A great chef and friend, Josh is a graduate of the New England Culinary Institute in Montpelier, Vermont, and he cooked with us at River Run for a while. As for these veggie burgers, even die-hard meat lovers like them. Including us.

2 pounds fresh spinach, well washed and drained
2 tablespoons unsalted butter
1 medium onion, peeled and chopped (about 1 cup)
½ pound button mushrooms, cleaned and minced (about 2 cups)
8 cloves garlic, peeled and minced
1½ cups Italian-style bread crumbs
½ cup grated Parmesan cheese
1 tablespoon salt, plus more for seasoning flour
2 teaspoons freshly ground black pepper, plus more for seasoning flour
Generous pinch cayenne pepper
7 egg whites, well chilled
½ cup all-purpose flour
2 tablespoons canola oil
Mayonnaise spiked with hot sauce, for serving

Remove and discard only the largest, toughest stems from the spinach. Pour several inches of water into a large pot, bring it to a boil, and put the spinach in a steamer basket or metal colander over the boiling water. Steam until well cooked, about 7 minutes.

Josh Grinker.

Remove the steamer basket or colander and allow the spinach to cool. Squeeze out as much water as possible, either by pressing the spinach in the colander or wrapping it in cheesecloth and squeezing or both. Chop the spinach and set it aside.

Heat a skillet over medium-high heat. Add the butter and reduce the heat to medium. Add the onion and mushrooms and cook, stirring, until just softened, 5 to 7 minutes. Add the garlic and cook a minute or two more. Scrape into a large bowl.

Add the spinach, bread crumbs, Parmesan, 1 tablespoon salt, 2 teaspoons black pepper, and pinch of cayenne to the mushroom mixture and stir to combine. Allow the mixture to cool to room temperature and mix again with your hands.

Whip the chilled egg whites until very stiff. (Chilled egg whites whip more easily.) Stir them gently into the mixture.

Put the flour in a shallow bowl and season with salt and black pepper to your liking. Using your hands, form the veggie mixture into 6 to 8 patties. Dredge in the seasoned flour (this step is optional but makes a nice crust). Heat the oil in a large skillet over medium heat and fry the patties on both sides until lightly browned. Serve with mayonnaise spiked with hot sauce.

Yield: 6 to 8 servings

CRAB CAKES

Along with Scrapple (page 83), this is another food Jimmy learned to love while spending weekends in Bethany Beach, Delaware. Crab cakes are as popular at River Run as they were with him and his buddies.

3 eggs
⅓ cup half-and-half
¾ cup mayonnaise
2½ tablespoons Dijon mustard
5 teaspoons Worcestershire sauce
3 green onions, trimmed and chopped
1 tablespoon Old Bay seasoning
2 cups cracker crumbs (40 to 50 saltines, crushed in food processor or
   with a rolling pin)
3 pounds crabmeat, carefully picked through, any shells discarded
1 cup all-purpose flour
1½ teaspoons salt
½ teaspoon freshly ground black pepper
½ teaspoon white pepper
Several tablespoons unsalted butter, for frying
Lemon slices and Tartar Sauce (page 174), for serving

Line a baking sheet with wax paper.
Beat the eggs in a large bowl and add the half-and-half, mayo, mustard, Worcestershire sauce, green onions, Old Bay seasoning, cracker crumbs, and crabmeat.

Mix well and, using your hands, form the mixture (it will be quite wet) into patties about ½ inch thick and 3 to 4 inches in diameter. Place on the prepared baking sheet and refrigerate for 1 to 2 hours.

In a shallow bowl, mix together the flour, salt, black pepper, and white pepper and set aside.

When you are ready to cook, remove the crab cakes from the fridge. Dredge both sides of the crab cakes by turning them in the seasoned flour.

Set the oven to warm. Line a baking sheet with a brown paper bag or paper towels.

Heat a skillet and melt enough butter to completely cover the bottom (2 to 3 tablespoons will cover the bottom of a 10- or 12-inch skillet). When butter has melted and is bubbling, add a few crab cakes at a time. Don't crowd the pan, or it will be hard to turn them over. Cook 4 to 5 minutes on each side, until they are golden brown. Remove the cakes from the pan and let them drain on the prepared baking sheet in the warm oven.

Wipe the pan lightly with a paper towel. Add more butter and let it melt and get hot, then add more cakes to the pan.

When all the crab cakes have been cooked, transfer them to a serving platter. Serve with lemon slices and tartar sauce.

Yield: sixteen 4-inch crab cakes, or about 8 servings

CATFISH CAKES

There are so many great ways to cook catfish. This is Maya's favorite.

2½ to 3 pounds catfish fillets
2 eggs, beaten
¾ cup mayonnaise
¼ cup half-and-half
2 tablespoons Dijon mustard
4½ teaspoons Worcestershire sauce
2½ teaspoons Old Bay seasoning
2 cups cracker crumbs (40 to 50 saltines, crushed in food processor or
    with a rolling pin)
2 or 3 dashes hot sauce
⅔ cup all-purpose flour
1½ teaspoons salt
½ teaspoon white pepper
Several tablespoons unsalted butter, for frying
Lemon slices and Tartar Sauce (page 174) or mayonnaise spiked with
    hot sauce, for serving

Cook the catfish fillets until done and set them aside. You can grill, fry, poach, broil, or bake them, as you like. To bake, put them in a lightly oiled baking pan in a 350-degree oven for about 15 minutes, turning them once about halfway through. Set the fish aside to cool.

Line a baking sheet with wax paper.

Combine the eggs, mayo, half-and-half, mustard, Worcestershire sauce, Old Bay seasoning, cracker crumbs, and hot sauce in a large bowl and blend well. When the fish has cooled enough to handle, chop or break it into the bowl and mix.

With your hands, form the mixture into 3- to 4-inch patties, place them on the lined baking sheet, and refrigerate for about half an hour.

When you are ready to cook, set your oven to warm. Line a baking sheet with a brown paper bag or paper towels.

Mix the flour, salt, and pepper in a shallow bowl. Dredge both sides of each catfish cake in the seasoned flour.

Heat a skillet and melt enough butter to completely cover the bottom (2 to 3 tablespoons will cover the bottom of a 10- or 12-inch skillet). When the butter has melted completely and is good and hot and bubbling, add a few catfish cakes to the skillet. Don't crowd the pan, or it will be hard to turn them over. Cook 4 to 5 minutes on each side, until they are golden brown. Remove the cakes from the pan and let them drain on the prepared baking sheet in the warm oven.

Wipe the pan lightly with a paper towel. Add more butter and let it melt and get hot, then add more cakes to the pan.

When all the catfish cakes have been cooked, transfer them to a serving platter. Serve them with lemon slices and the garnish of your choice.

Yield: about twelve 4-inch catfish cakes, or 4 to 6 servings

THE JOY OF FRYING

Frying foods is, without a doubt, Jimmy's favorite way to cook and to eat. Maybe that's because Jimmy's mother is the best fry cook of all time. She's been deep-frying chicken, catfish, beef, venison, vegetables, apple pies, and just about everything else for as long as Jimmy can remember.

Deep-frying seemed to fall out of favor several years ago. People started ordering and cooking grilled and steamed foods instead of the tasty deep-fried versions. While grilled and steamed foods are also delicious (and probably a little healthier), it's hard to beat a big ol' platter of fried chicken or catfish.

The major trick to frying foods is getting the oil hot enough (325 to 350 degrees) and keeping it at a constant temperature. When this is done, the oil does not soak into the food but seals the batter around it, helping to retain natural flavor and juices. The oil should be what the food is cooked in, not part of it.

So don't be afraid to fry. All the fried recipes in this book have been tested in a home kitchen using plain, ordinary kitchen utensils. What you need for frying is a Dutch oven, a good pair of tongs, and a candy/fry thermometer for determining when the oil is hot enough and—just as important—keeping it at a constant temperature. Have a lot of oil on hand (Jimmy uses canola) and a lot of brown paper bags or paper towels for draining the food after it's fried.

Another thing you need is patience. Frying food is a little like watching that pot that never boils; it almost always takes longer than you think. But don't be tempted to turn away from your task—that's the very minute when the food will go from brown to burned.

Lucy Huttemann and Art Huttemann with family: Lisa, Steve, Kaitlin, and Justin Folsom. Loyal customers and friends.

When you're through frying and the oil has cooled, strain it and use it again. Unless you've fried something really strong—like fish—the oil should be odorless and completely reusable. When it starts to darken and takes on a strong odor, pour it back into its empty bottle, cap it, and throw it out.

CHICKEN-FRIED HAMBURGER STEAK WITH ONIONS & GRAVY

A chicken-fried steak is a steak dredged in seasoned flour and fried. A hamburger steak with onions and gravy is a truck-stop favorite and was a house specialty at Mistillis's, a now-closed but well-remembered restaurant favored by students at Ole Miss. (Mistillis's also served a mean gumbo.) The idea to chicken-fry a hamburger patty came to Jimmy when he was experimenting with making a deep-fried hamburger for sandwiches. As soon he breaded the patty, he was reminded of chicken-fried steak. The onions and gravy followed naturally.

For the gravy:
2 cups beef stock or canned broth
2 cups half-and-half
½ cup all-purpose flour
1½ tablespoons Worcestershire sauce
1 teaspoon salt
1 teaspoon freshly ground black pepper
½ teaspoon garlic powder

For the hamburger and onions:
Canola oil, for frying (1½ to 2 cups)
2 large onions, peeled and sliced

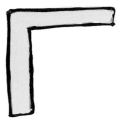

3 pounds ground beef
2 cups all-purpose flour
1 tablespoon salt
2 teaspoons freshly ground black pepper
1 teaspoon garlic powder

Make the gravy first: In a saucepan, heat the stock (or broth) and 3 cups of the half-and-half to almost boiling. In a small bowl, combine the remaining cup of half-and-half with the flour, blending them with a whisk until smooth (no lumps!). Slowly add this mixture to the simmering broth, whisking constantly until the gravy thickens. Add the Worcestershire sauce, salt, pepper, and garlic powder. Stir the gravy again and set aside.

Joseph Kennedy, Jimmy's brother and Josie's namesake.

Line a platter with paper towels.

Heat a couple of tablespoons of the oil in a large cast-iron skillet and, when hot, add the onions and sauté until it begins to soften, 5 to 7 minutes. Remove the onion with a slotted spoon and set aside on the lined platter.

Form the ground beef into 4 large patties, about 12 ounces each.

Mix the flour in a shallow bowl with the salt, pepper, and garlic powder.

Dredge the hamburger patties in the seasoned flour mixture, patting some on with your hands until they are well coated.

Meanwhile, pour about a ½ inch of oil into the skillet and heat over medium-high heat until very hot but not smoking (the surface should look wavy).

When the oil is hot, gently slip 2 of the dredged hamburger steaks into the oil. Cook for 5 to 10 minutes on each side, depending on how rare you like your meat. As they are done, remove and drain on the lined platter.

Reheat the gravy.

To serve, plate the hamburger steak, spoon the onion on top, and ladle on a generous portion of gravy. If this isn't enough fat for you, you can always melt cheese on the steak and then spoon the gravy on top!

Yield: 4 humungous servings

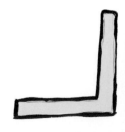

MEAT LOAF

Use the leftovers (if there are any) for sandwiches the next day. Makes a great filling for Omelets (page 75) too.

1 tablespoon unsalted butter
1 medium onion, peeled and chopped (about 1 cup)
1 medium green bell pepper, seeded and chopped (about 1 cup)
1 small stalk celery, trimmed and chopped (about ½ cup)
1 tablespoon minced garlic
1 pound ground beef
½ pound ground pork, loose sausage, or finely chopped andouille sausage
1 cup Corn Bread crumbs (page 60), bread crumbs, crushed saltines, or
    crushed corn flakes
1 teaspoon salt
½ teaspoon white pepper
½ teaspoon dried basil
¼ teaspoon dried thyme
2 teaspoons Dry BBQ Rub (page 195; optional, but good)
1 tablespoon Worcestershire sauce
½ cup milk
2 eggs, beaten
½ cup BBQ Sauce (page 196)

Set the oven to 375 degrees.

Melvin Chase, high school coach and mailman.

Melt the butter in a skillet over medium-high heat and, when it's good and hot, sauté the onion, bell pepper, celery, and garlic until they begin to soften, 5 to 7 minutes. Set aside to cool.

In a large bowl, mix together the meats, crumbs, salt, pepper, herbs, BBQ rub, Worcestershire sauce, milk, eggs, and ¼ cup of the BBQ sauce. When the vegetables have cooled well enough to handle, put them in the bowl and mix everything together with your hands.

Place the meat loaf in a baking pan—a 9-by-5-inch loaf pan works well—and pat it into shape. Pour the remaining ¼ cup BBQ sauce over the top, spreading it evenly.

Bake, uncovered, for 45 minutes to an hour.

Yield: about 6 servings

☆ SLOPPY JOES

These are even better than the ones you remember from Boy (or Girl) Scouts. Serve over Grit Cakes (page 43) or toast with eggs for breakfast; over sliced white bread or buns for lunch or supper.

2 pounds ground beef
1 tablespoon canola oil
2 medium onions, peeled and chopped (about 2 cups)
1 cup ketchup
1 cup BBQ Sauce (page 196)
2 tablespoons Worcestershire sauce
2 tablespoons brown sugar
2 tablespoons cider vinegar
1 tablespoon dry mustard
Salt, to taste
Freshly ground black pepper, to taste
Water, beer, or canned beef broth, as needed

Rick Clark, woodworker and former River Run cook.

Heat a large, heavy skillet or Dutch oven over medium-high heat. Put in the ground beef and brown it, stirring often. Drain and discard the drippings.

Meanwhile, heat the oil in a separate skillet and cook the onions until they are soft, 7 to 10 minutes. Add the cooked onions and remaining ingredients to the cooked ground beef and bring to a simmer. If the mixture isn't wet enough for you, add a little water, beer, or beef broth until you get the perfect amount of sloppiness you desire. Cook, with the skillet mostly covered, for about 20 minutes, adding more liquid if needed. Make sure everything is heated through before serving.

Yield: about 6 servings

STEAK WITH WHISKEY SAUCE

This recipe gives you a use for the bourbon that's been sitting in the pantry for months, or you can look at it as a good excuse to go out and buy a bottle. It also gives you a good way to dress up steak for company. We think porterhouse steaks are a good choice here.

2 steaks (about 12 ounces each)
Salt, to taste
Freshly ground black pepper, to taste
Canola oil, for cooking (about 2 tablespoons for a 12-inch skillet)
¼ to ½ pound (as you like) button mushrooms, cleaned and sliced (1 to 2 cups)
2 shallots, peeled and chopped, or ½ medium onion, peeled and chopped (about ½ cup)
1 teaspoon minced garlic
½ pint bourbon, plus a bit more if needed
¼ cup heavy cream, plus a bit more if needed

In this recipe, you will sear the steaks in a skillet but finish cooking them on a grill, under a broiler, or in another pan. Decide how you want to finish the cooking and get set up (i.e., preheat the grill or broiler) in good time for finishing the dish.

Sprinkle the steaks with salt and pepper. Heat a large skillet (a 12-incher works well). When hot, add enough oil to just coat the bottom. When almost

Crow's Lunch,
pre–River Run.

smoking, sear the steaks on both sides. If the pan is good and hot, this will take less than a minute per side.

Remove the steaks and set them aside on a platter. Reduce heat to medium-high. Toss the mushrooms, shallots (or onions) and garlic into the skillet and cook, stirring, until they start to soften. If they begin to stick, add a little more oil—move the vegetables to one side, tilt the pan, and pour in a teaspoon or two. Let it get hot before you continue cooking.

Pour in the bourbon and let it come to a boil. Immediately reduce the heat and add the cream. Pour in any steak juices that have collected on the plate holding the steaks. Simmer until the sauce reduces to a consistency you like; this will probably take somewhere between 10 and 20 minutes. Taste and add more salt and pepper if needed. Likewise, you can add a bit more bourbon and cream as the sauce cooks.

This is a good time to throw the steaks on a grill, into a pan, or under a broiler and cook them to your liking.

When the steaks are done, let them rest for a few minutes. Slice and serve with the sauce on top.

Yield: 2 hefty servings

106

CORNED BEEF HASH

An all-time breakfast favorite. You can substitute roast beef, steak, chicken, turkey, venison or any other meat, poultry or fish for the corned beef.

¾ pound potatoes (1½ to 2 large), scrubbed and chopped (about 3 cups)
½ pound thick-cut lean smoked bacon, chopped
2 medium onions, peeled and chopped (about 2 cups)
1 medium green bell pepper, seeded and chopped (about 1 cup)
1 small stalk celery, trimmed and chopped (about ½ cup)
1 pound cooked corned beef, chopped (about 4 cups)
1 teaspoon dried thyme
1 teaspoon dried basil
½ teaspoon white pepper
Salt, to taste
Freshly ground black pepper, to taste
Eggs (cooked to your liking) and toast, for serving

Put the potatoes in a pot and cover them with cold water. Put the pot over medium-high heat, cover, and bring to a boil. Cook until just tender (start checking them at 10 minutes). Drain and set aside.

Line a plate with paper towels.

In a heavy 10-inch skillet, fry the bacon until done but not crispy. Remove it from the skillet and drain on the lined plate. Drain and save the bacon grease.

Return 1 tablespoon of the reserved bacon grease to the skillet, put the skillet over medium heat, and cook the onions, bell pepper, and celery, stirring often, until they start to soften, 5 to 7 minutes.

Put the sautéed vegetables in a large mixing bowl. Add the corned beef, the reserved potatoes and bacon, thyme, basil, and white pepper. Season with salt and pepper. Stir gently or mix with your hands until everything is well blended.

To cook the hash, heat a couple of tablespoons of the reserved bacon grease in the skillet over medium-high heat. Add the hash; it will fill the skillet. This hash will be loose; it won't form a solid "pancake" like the canned kind, so you can't flip it over as a whole. Instead, cook the hash undisturbed until a crust begins to form on one side, then flip sections of it over with a spatula so that the sides brown evenly.

Serve with eggs and toast of your choice.

Yield: 4 servings

Cameron Cope, carpenter.

108

FRIED CHICKEN

Fried chicken could easily be considered the "universal dish," common to just about every country. We think that deep-fried chicken with a golden brown, crispy batter on the outside and tender, juicy meat inside is hard to beat. Since you want to serve the chicken as soon as it's done, make sure you have any other components of the meal—veggies or potatoes or what have you—ready to go.

Canola oil, for frying (about 10 cups for a 4-quart Dutch oven)
2 cups buttermilk
2 cups all-purpose flour
1 tablespoon salt
1 tablespoon coarsely ground black pepper
1½ teaspoons garlic powder
1 whole frying chicken (3 to 4 pounds), cut up

Set the oven to warm. Line a baking sheet with a brown paper bag or paper towels.

Heat 2 to 3 inches of oil in a Dutch oven until it reaches 325 to 350 degrees on a deep-fry thermometer.

While the oil is heating, pour the buttermilk into a shallow bowl.

In another bowl, combine the flour, salt, pepper, and garlic powder.

Dip the chicken pieces in the buttermilk, then dredge them in the seasoned flour, patting the flour on with your fingers so it makes a good coating.

Using tongs, carefully place 3 or 4 of the coated chicken pieces in the hot oil and cook for 8 to 10 minutes. Then, using the tongs, move the chicken around in the oil and cook another 8 to 10 minutes. Keep an eye on the temperature of the oil and adjust the heat so that it remains steady.

Again using the tongs, lift one piece of chicken at a time out of the oil and hold it over the pot so it can drain a little; then set it on the prepared baking sheet to drain. Slice a piece to make sure it is cooked through; if still pink inside, return it to the oil. When the pieces are cooked, let them drain on the lined baking sheet and keep them warm in the oven while you fry the remaining pieces.

Serve ASAP.

Yield: 4 to 6 servings

FRIED CHICKEN SALAD WITH BUTTERMILK DRESSING

This is one of the most requested lunch dishes at River Run. There's something about the combination of slightly tart buttermilk dressing and golden, crispy chicken that appeals to a lot of people.

2 cups buttermilk
4 boneless, skinless chicken breast halves
2 cups all-purpose flour
2 teaspoons salt
2 teaspoons freshly ground black pepper
1 teaspoon garlic powder
Canola oil, for frying (about 10 cups for a 4-quart Dutch oven)
½ head romaine lettuce, rinsed and drained and torn into small pieces
½ head red leaf lettuce, rinsed and drained and torn into small pieces
1 red bell pepper, seeded and chopped (about 1 cup)
½ onion, peeled and chopped (about ½ cup)
½ to ⅔ cup Buttermilk Dressing (page 193)

Set the oven to warm. Line a baking sheet with a brown paper bag or paper towels.

Pour the buttermilk over the chicken in a bowl and let it soak a few minutes.

In a shallow dish, mix together the flour, salt, pepper, and garlic powder. Remove the chicken breasts from the buttermilk and dredge in the seasoned flour on both sides, pressing the mixture on with your fingers so they are well coated.

Heat 2 to 3 inches of oil in a heavy-bottomed pan or Dutch oven until it reaches 325 to 350 degrees on a deep-fry thermometer. Using tongs, fry the coated chicken breasts, 2 at a time, until they are a deep golden brown on all sides, 12 to 15 minutes. (Slice into the chicken to make sure it is not pink in the middle; if it is, return it to the oil. It might get quite dark on the outside, but that's OK as long as it doesn't burn.) Drain on the prepared baking sheet and keep warm in the oven while you fry the remaining chicken. As you work, keep an eye on the temperature of the oil and adjust the heat so that it remains steady.

Divide the lettuce, bell pepper, and onion, among 4 plates. Top each salad with 1 sliced chicken breast and a generous dollop of dressing.

Yield: 4 servings

Clara Mamet.

CHICKEN & DUMPLINGS

This is Jimmy's second-favorite way to eat chicken, deep-fried being the first. Chicken & Dumplings is the classic one-dish meal. You can also save a meaty ham bone from Christmas or Easter dinner and use the same steps to make Ham & Dumplings. With either dish, using self-rising flour is critical; we've been fooling around with substitutions but can't get quite the spongy "dumpling" texture Jimmy remembers from childhood.

1 whole frying chicken (3 to 3½ pounds)
1 large onion, peeled and quartered
4 carrots, peeled and quartered
4 to 6 stalks celery, trimmed and coarsely chopped
4 to 6 cloves garlic, peeled and halved
2 or 3 bay leaves
Salt

A dozen or so peppercorns
3½ cups self-rising flour
1½ cups milk
2 eggs, beaten
Freshly ground black pepper, to taste (optional)
A small handful minced parsley or other fresh herbs, for flavoring dumplings and for serving (optional)
1 tablespoon unsalted butter

Put the chicken, onion, carrots, celery, garlic, bay leaves, at least 1 tablespoon salt, and peppercorns into a 6-quart (or larger) pot and cover with cold water. Bring to a boil.

Reduce the heat to a simmer and cook until the chicken is falling off the bone, about 1½ hours. Remove the chicken from the broth and allow it to cool. As soon as the chicken is cool enough to handle, take the skin off and discard it, then take the meat off the bones and return the bones to the broth and cook for another hour or two. Meanwhile, refrigerate the meat until needed.

When the broth has cooked, taste for seasoning and add more salt if needed. When the broth is good and tasty, remove it from the heat and let it cool. It is best if you can wait overnight so that you can skim the congealed fat off the top. If time is short, put the broth in your refrigerator for an hour or two and skim. Or just skim what you can off the hot broth (remember: Fat is flavor).

Strain the broth through a fine-mesh strainer or cheesecloth. Return the broth to the pot and discard the vegetables and bay leaves.

To make the dumplings, mix 3 cups of the flour, ½ teaspoon salt, ½ cup of the milk, ½ cup of the chicken broth, and the eggs. If you like, you can also add some pepper and parsley or other fresh herbs to the dough. The dough will be fairly sticky.

Dust a work surface with the remaining ½ cup flour. Knead the dough on the board, working in this extra flour. Roll the dough to about ⅛-inch thick. Cut the dough into strips about 1-inch wide. If the strips are too long for your pot, just cut them in half or quarters. When the dumplings are all cut, move them apart on the board and let them dry for 15 to 20 minutes.

While the dumplings are drying, heat the broth to a low simmer. Add the remaining cup of milk and taste again for seasoning. Return the chicken meat to the broth.

Place the dumpling strips side by side in the broth, then crosswise, if needed. Cut the butter into tiny pieces and scatter across the top of the dumplings. Cook, uncovered, until the dumplings are tender and cooked through,

30 to 45 minutes. Resist the temptation to poke the dumplings down into the broth.

Serve a healthy portion of meat, broth, and dumplings in large bowls or deep dinner plates. Garnish with fresh herbs if desired.

Yield: 6 to 8 servings

Susan Thomas, writer and gardener; Peter Sills, writer

MAYA'S MOM'S CHICKEN & RICE

Fortunately for us, we get to eat dinner at Charlotte's house quite often, and this is one of the dishes we are always hoping she makes. While her recipe calls for a cut-up whole chicken, we usually use just thighs.

½ teaspoon saffron threads (optional, but nice)

2 cups hot chicken stock, canned broth, or bouillon

2 tablespoons olive oil

1 small frying chicken (about 3½ pounds), cut up, or 3 to 4 pounds chicken pieces

1 medium onion, peeled and coarsely chopped (about 1 cup)

2 cloves garlic, peeled and minced

2 slices fresh ginger, peeled and minced

1 red bell pepper, seeded and coarsely chopped (about 1 cup)

¼ pound button mushrooms, cleaned and sliced (about 1 cup)

1 cup chopped broccoli florets, zucchini, or other green vegetable

1½ cups uncooked brown rice

Charlotte Potok, potter. When Mom cooks, we listen.

116

1 cup dry white wine
Salt, to taste
Freshly ground black pepper, to taste

Set the oven to 350 degrees.

Sprinkle the saffron threads (if using) over the heated broth to soak.

Heat the oil over medium heat in a large skillet. Cook the chicken until it begins to brown—5 to 7 minutes—turning over about halfway through. Remove from the pan and set aside on a plate.

Add the onion, garlic, ginger, bell pepper, mushrooms, and broccoli (or other vegetable) to the skillet and stir-fry lightly, about 3 minutes. Add the rice and cook, stirring, for 2 minutes. Remove the mixture from the skillet and spread evenly in a 13-by-9-inch baking dish. Add the stock and wine, stirring gently to distribute evenly. Place the chicken, skin side up, on top of the rice-vegetable mixture, pouring in any juices that have accumulated on the plate. Season with salt and pepper.

Bake about 1 hour, or the until the chicken is crispy and the rice is tender. (A glass baking pan will require 15 to 20 minutes longer in the oven.)

Yield: 4 to 6 servings

Steve Bogart.

FIVE-FLAVOR CHICKEN

For years after we moved to Vermont, we kept hearing about Steve Bogart and his wonderful Chinese food. When we finally met, it was to see if he wanted to open up River Run at night as his own place. He did, and he turned our waitress station/freezer area into a small, efficient, and professional Chinese kitchen. We had a great time for a year as River Run by day and A Single Pebble by night. Steve and A Single Pebble are now located in nearby Berlin, Vermont.

1 whole frying chicken (about 3 pounds)

1 bunch green onions, trimmed

5 slices fresh ginger

2 tablespoons dry sherry

1 tablespoon plus 1 teaspoon minced garlic

1 tablespoon plus 1 teaspoon minced ginger

3 tablespoons minced green onions

1 tablespoon minced bamboo shoots

1 tablespoon minced water chestnuts

1 tablespoon minced carrot

1 tablespoon minced mushrooms (see note)

3 tablespoons soy sauce

1 tablespoon sugar

1 teaspoon Asian chili paste

2 teaspoons tahini or peanut butter

2 teaspoons vegetable oil

½ large head iceberg lettuce, shredded

Minced fresh cilantro, for serving

Toasted sesame seeds, for serving

In a large pot, bring 3 to 4 quarts of water to a boil. Put the chicken in and simmer, covered, for 30 minutes. Take the pot off the heat, keep the lid on, and wrap the pot in a large bath towel. Let the pot stand for another 30 minutes. This is called "white cooking," a Chinese poaching method that leaves the meat very white and tender. (You can skip the bath towel wrap and just let the pot sit off the heat for 30 minutes, but wrapping improves the texture.)

When the time is up, remove the chicken from the pot and allow it to cool. Save the stock.

When the chicken is cool, shred it by hand, discarding the skin. Put the meat in a colander and refrigerate. Put the bones back in the pot. Add the whole green onions, ginger slices, and sherry to the pot and simmer, covered, for 1 hour.

Meanwhile, assemble the sauce ingredients. In a small bowl, mix 1 tablespoon of each: garlic, ginger, green onions, bamboo shoots, water chestnuts, carrot, and mushrooms. In another small bowl, mix the remaining teaspoon garlic, remaining teaspoon ginger, remaining 2 tablespoons green onion, and the soy, sugar, chili paste, and tahini (or peanut butter).

In a wok or small skillet, heat the vegetable oil until smoking. Add the first bowl of ingredients (with bamboo shoots) and stir-fry until fragrant (this will take only a minute or so). Add the second bowl (with tahini) and bring to a boil. Add a bit of stock from the pot, one teaspoon at a time, to bring the sauce to the consistency you desire.

Place the chicken, in its colander, back in the hot stock. Do not cook the chicken; the aim is just to reheat it.

Drain the heated chicken and place it on a bed of shredded lettuce. Top with the sauce. Garnish with minced cilantro and sprinkle with sesame seeds.

The stock left over is too good to waste. Save it for making a soup or for another purpose. If you can't use it right away, freeze it for future use. (Ice cube trays are handy for freezing in small amounts.)

Note: Use dried black Chinese mushrooms (shiitakes) soaked in hot water for 20 minutes before mincing (remove and discard the tough stems). You can substitute domestic button mushrooms or just leave them out altogether.

Yield: 4 main-course servings

FRIED CATFISH

For as long as Jimmy can remember, everyone close to him—his dad, when he was alive, his mother, brothers, uncles, aunts, and friends—has been catching, cooking, and eating catfish. Whether it was wild catfish caught out of the creeks and sloughs or the fish they raised in small ponds in the pasture, Jimmy's family had catfish on their table at least two or three times a week, and Jimmy always looked forward to it. All through high school and college, he and his buddies ran trotlines and held big catfish fries. After college he worked as a legislative assistant for Congressman Webb Franklin from Mississippi's Second District. At the time the district represented almost 90 percent of the catfish farming industry and pretty much set the standard. After his stint on Capitol Hill, Jimmy moved to New York City and started peddling Mississippi farm-raised catfish to restaurants there. After he met Maya, they moved to her hometown of Plainfield, Vermont, and opened River Run. He's now cooking and serving catfish to New Englanders and is happy to say he's made catfish fans of quite a few. Seems Jimmy can't get away from catfish—and wouldn't want to. This basic recipe is the one he has known since childhood.

2 cups buttermilk
4 cups coarse-ground yellow
   cornmeal
4 cups crushed corn flakes
1 tablespoon salt
1 tablespoon coarsely ground
   black pepper
1½ teaspoons garlic powder

Canola oil, for frying (about 10
   cups for a 4-quart Dutch
   oven)
8 catfish fillets (about 8 ounces
   each)
Lemon wedges and Tartar Sauce
   (page 174), for serving

Pour the buttermilk into a shallow bowl.

In another shallow bowl, combine the cornmeal, corn flakes, salt, pepper, and garlic powder.

Set the oven to warm. Line a baking sheet with a brown paper bag or paper towels.

Heat 2 to 3 inches of oil in a Dutch oven to 325 to 350 degrees.

While the oil is heating, dip the catfish fillets into the buttermilk and then dredge them in the seasoned cornmeal, patting the mixture on with your fingers to coat the fillets well.

Using tongs, carefully lower the catfish fillets into the oil. Cook 2 at a time. Keep an eye on the temperature of the oil as you work, adjusting the heat to keep it constant. Fry the catfish until a deep golden brown—the tail ends will curl up and turn a slightly darker color than the rest of the fish. This should take 8 to 10 minutes. Drain on the prepared baking sheet and keep warm in the oven while you fry the remaining fillets.

Serve with lemon wedges and tartar sauce.

Yield: 8 servings

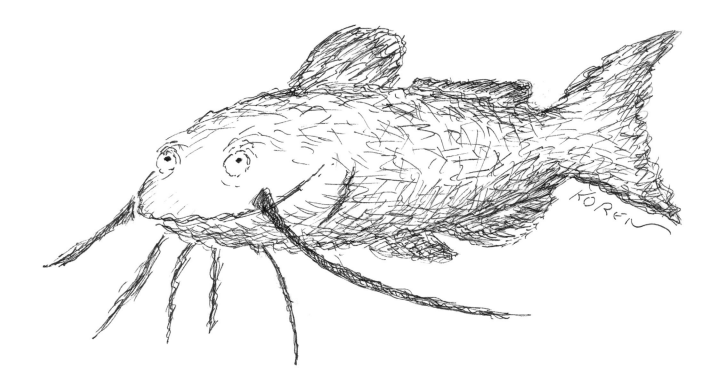

Curtis, Ben, and Ed Koren.

123

SQUIRREL FISH

Here's a variation on Fried Catfish (page 121) from our friend Steve Bogart, who cooks extraordinary Chinese food at *A Single Pebble* in Berlin, Vermont, and who ran his restaurant at night out of River Run for about a year. He says that this dish got its name because the fish chatters much like a squirrel when it is cooking. It does, too.

For the fish:
2 catfish fillets (8 to 10 ounces each)
½ cup cornstarch
⅓ cup all-purpose flour

For the sauce:
4½ teaspoons finely minced garlic
4½ teaspoons finely minced fresh ginger
7 tablespoons minced green onions
6 tablespoons minced bamboo shoots
6 tablespoons minced water chestnuts
3 tablespoons minced red bell pepper
3 tablespoons minced green bell pepper
¾ cup ketchup
3 tablespoons dry sherry
3 tablespoons soy sauce
1 tablespoon sugar
1 teaspoon Asian chili paste, or to taste

1½ teaspoons Asian sesame oil (made with toasted sesame seeds), plus
   more for serving
4½ teaspoons cornstarch
3 tablespoons water
Vegetable oil
Chopped fresh cilantro, for serving

Place a catfish fillet, skin side down, on a cutting board. Holding your knife at a 45-degree angle to the fillet, make 5 slices along the length of the fish, not cutting through but making flaps. Repeat for the second fillet. Set aside.

In a shallow dish, combine the cornstarch and flour and mix well. Dredge the fish in the cornstarch mixture and set it aside.

Assemble the sauce ingredients: First, get out 4 small bowls. In the first bowl, mix the garlic, ginger, and 1 tablespoon of the minced green onions. In the second bowl, mix the remaining 6 tablespoons green onions, the bamboo shoots, water chestnuts, and bell peppers. In the third bowl, mix the ketchup, sherry, soy sauce, sugar, chili paste, and sesame oil. In the fourth bowl, mix the cornstarch and water. Set the 4 bowls aside.

Line a platter with paper towels.

Heat 4 cups oil in a wok until it reaches 325 to 350 degrees on a deep-fry thermometer. (If you use a Dutch oven or other kind of pot instead, you may need quite a bit more oil; you want at least 3 inches of oil in the pot.) Using tongs, slowly lower a floured fillet into the oil and cook for about 8 to 10 minutes, until crispy. Remove it with tongs or a slotted spoon and set it aside on the lined platter to drain. Repeat for the remaining fillet.

While the fish is frying, make the sauce: Heat another wok or a skillet, add 1 to 2 tablespoons of oil, and heat. Add the first bowl of ingredients (with garlic and ginger), stirring for a minute or so until fragrant. Add the second bowl (with bamboo shoots) and then the third (the ketchup mixture), mixing and cooking briefly. At the end, add the fourth bowl (cornstarch and water) and stir until the sauce thickens enough to drape off a ladle.

Place the fried fish on a platter, pour the sauce over, drizzle with sesame oil, and sprinkle with chopped cilantro.

Yield: 2 main-course servings: more when served in the Chinese manner, in combination with other dishes

CATFISH JAMBALAYA

This recipe won the 1996 Catfish Institute's Restaurant Award, which was given to ten restaurants nationwide. It's got a lot going for it: it's easy, you can make it ahead of time, it feeds a lot of people, and it's kind of special.

1 pound andouille sausage or kielbasa, cut into 1-inch pieces (see note)

1 pound ham, in a chunk (not sliced), cut into 1-inch pieces

2 medium onions, peeled and chopped (about 2 cups)

1 medium green bell pepper, seeded and chopped (about 1 cup)

3 small stalks celery, trimmed and chopped (about 1½ cups)

1 clove garlic, peeled and minced

One 28-ounce can whole tomatoes, with juice

1½ teaspoons dried thyme

1 teaspoon dried oregano

1 teaspoon freshly ground black pepper

1 teaspoon white pepper

1 teaspoon cayenne pepper

½ teaspoon dried basil

7 cups fish or chicken stock, canned chicken broth, or fish
   or chicken broth made from bouillon

1¾ cups uncooked white rice

3 pounds catfish fillets, cut into 1-inch pieces

Chopped green onions, for garnish (optional)

Jimmy and Lake Champlain catfish.

Heat a heavy-bottomed pot or Dutch oven over medium-high heat. Add the sausage pieces and cook, turning, until lightly browned. Add the ham and continue cooking for 10 to 15 minutes.

Add the onions, bell peppers, celery, and garlic and stir to mix; continue cooking for another 10 to 15 minutes. Add the tomatoes (and juice) and seasonings, stir to mix, and cook for 5 to 10 minutes, stirring and chopping up the tomatoes with your spoon as you stir.

Add the stock (or broth or bouillon) and simmer, with the pot mostly covered, for 1 hour. Add the rice and cook, stirring occasionally, for 25 to 30 minutes. The rice should be tender and should have absorbed most of the cooking liquid. The jambalaya should be pretty thick, not soupy. Cook a bit longer, if needed.

Now add the catfish, stir gently, and cook for about 10 more minutes, or until the catfish is cooked through (slice a piece to check). Be careful when stirring the jambalaya so that the catfish doesn't break up too much. Taste for salt and spices and add any more that you want.

Serve on rimmed dinner plates or in shallow soup bowls. Garnish with chopped green onions, if desired.

Note: Kielbasa is much less spicy than andouille sausage; if you use it, you might want to increase the amount of pepper (cayenne, black, and white).

Yield: about 10 servings

HORSERADISH-CRUSTED FISH

This recipe is from Trevis Gleason, who cooked with us for a while and who also helped us create the recipe for River Run Hot Sauce. Horseradish lovers will be in heaven. Delicious with Mashed Potatoes (page 159).

1 cup grated fresh horseradish root, or 16 ounces prepared
  horseradish (see note)
2 cups unseasoned bread crumbs
½ teaspoon dried thyme
½ teaspoon dried parsley
½ teaspoon dried oregano
Salt, to taste
Freshly ground black pepper, to taste
2 cups all-purpose flour
3 eggs, beaten
4 firm fish fillets: catfish, grouper, snapper, or haddock (8 to 10
  ounces each)
Canola oil, for cooking (2 to 3 tablespoons for a 10-inch skillet)

If using prepared horseradish, dump it into a sieve over a sink and use a spoon or your hands to squeeze out as much excess moisture as possible. The idea is to get it the consistency of fresh horseradish root. You should have about 1 cup.

Trevis Gleason.

In a shallow bowl, mix the horseradish, bread crumbs, thyme, parsley, oregano, salt, and pepper.

Put the flour in one shallow bowl and the eggs in another.

Dredge each fish fillet in flour on both sides, then dip the flesh side of the fillet in the egg. Dredge the dipped flesh side of the fish in the horseradish mixture, using your fingers to pat on a good coating.

Set the oven to warm.

Coat the bottom of a heavy skillet with oil and heat over medium heat. Pan-fry the horseradish side of the fish until quite brown, about 4 to 6 minutes. Flip and brown the skin side, also about 4 to 6 minutes. Keep the cooked fillets warm in the oven while you finish with the others.

Note: Try to buy a prepared horseradish that contains only horseradish root, vinegar, and salt and not a lot of other additives. Also, prepared horseradish tends to be salty, so don't add too much salt.

Yield: 4 servings

BAKED BLUEFISH

The fresher the bluefish, the better. If bluefish is out of season, you can use catfish or any other white fish. I've seen variations of this recipe using mayonnaise instead of sour cream, and the bluefish always turns out tasty.

> 1½ to 2 pounds bluefish fillets
> ⅔ cup sour cream
> 1 medium red onion, peeled and grated or minced (about 1 cup)
> Salt, to taste
> Freshly ground black pepper, to taste

Set the oven to 350 degrees.

Lightly grease a baking dish large enough to hold the fillets in a single layer. Place the fillets in the dish, skin side down. Cover them evenly with the sour cream and then sprinkle with the onion. The sour cream and onion should make a fairly thick layer on the fillets. Sprinkle salt and pepper on top and bake for 25 minutes, then place under the broiler for 5 to 7 minutes.

Yield: 4 to 6 servings

Jimmy in the kitchen.

BBQ

There's been plenty written, much discussion, and more than a little controversy about barbecue. But there is one thing that all BBQ-ers worth their sauce will agree on, and that is, simply, theirs is the best.

To define our terms, BBQ is basically the same as hot-smoking, which means cooking food at a temperature of around 175 to 250 degrees for a long time. The smoke and heat are either generated from a separate firebox or from a very low hardwood fire right under the food.

There are many styles of BBQ: Carolina, Texas, Kansas City, and Memphis style among them. At River Run our BBQ style would probably best be described as Memphis style, which uses a dry rub during the long, slow cooking time and a sweet, sometimes spicy tomato-based BBQ sauce mopped on after cooking, mixed in with, or just served alongside the meat.

132

At River Run we do BBQ on Thursday and Friday nights in the summer—eat-in or take-out. Customers are always after us to expand our BBQ nights, and we just might.

Our smoker at the restaurant is a jury-rigged outfit that combines an electric caterer's oven and a small woodstove. The woodstove is outside; the oven hangs—half in and half out—from a kitchen window. We fire up the woodstove, and the smoke travels up a pipe to the oven. Because the smoke alone brings the temperature in the oven to about 200 degrees (perfect for slow, hot smoking), we never even have to plug the oven in. It's a funny-looking rig, but it works great. The point is that it doesn't take much to make a smoker. Jimmy put ours together in a couple of hours one afternoon with the help of two friends: his hunting and fishing buddy, Conrad Dix, and Josh Grinker, a chef who used to cook with us. If you don't want to go to the trouble of building your own rig, almost all stores that sell gas or charcoal grills sell smokers or smoker/grills, which are grills that can be fitted with separate fireboxes.

Another alternative is to forget the smoking and just use your oven. Purists will disagree, but you can make BBQ to be proud of—ribs, pulled pork, chicken, or what have you—right in your own kitchen. You won't have as much smoky flavor, but the results are still going to be delicious. Use the dry rub while the meat slow-cooks, then finish the meat off on the grill or under the broiler, if need be, and serve it with homemade sauce.

One of the great things about BBQ is that it's almost impossible to go wrong. Nearly everyone likes the taste of slow-cooked meat and a tasty sauce.

Another great thing about BBQ is developing your own style and method. Don't be afraid to experiment. Of course, it will be hard to equal the results here at River Run. Because we know for sure that our BBQ is the BEST.

Note: Our recipe for BBQ Sauce is on page 196. To order River Run BBQ Sauce already bottled, see page xx.

River Run diehards: Debbie Ardamendo, Bob Prince, Greg Hanson, Jed Clifford, Mark René Broussard, Rachel Prince.

PULLED PORK

In many regions of the South, this dish defines barbecue. At River Run we call it "meat candy." It's traditionally smoked, but a low, slow oven will work. Serve as dinner with Mashed Potatoes (page 159) and Collards (page 168) or for lunch as a sandwich on a white roll with Maya's Slaw (page 153) spooned on top of the meat.

    5 pounds fresh (*not* smoked) pork butt, bone-in (look for the cut sold
        as "Boston butt"), trimmed of any visible fat
    ¼ cup Dry BBQ Rub (page 195)
    3 cups BBQ Sauce (page 196), plus several cups more for serving

Set the oven to 250 degrees.

Line a baking pan large enough to hold the pork with heavy-duty aluminum foil (this makes cleaning up easier). Put the meat on the foil and sprinkle the dry rub evenly over it. (Despite its name, *don't* rub it in.) Cover the pan with a tent of heavy-duty aluminum foil; fold over the edges to seal. Slow-roast 8 to 9 hours; you know the meat is done when you poke at it with a fork and it falls off the bone.

Allow the meat to cool enough so that you can handle it. Using your hands, shred the meat, discarding any fat.

Heat 3 cups BBQ sauce in a saucepan; mix in the shredded meat. Serve warm on a dinner plate or on a sandwich roll, with extra warm BBQ sauce on the side.

Yield: at least 12 servings

COUNTRY-STYLE SPARE RIBS

Country-style spare ribs are not actually ribs. They are cut from either the loin or the butt of the pork, so they sort of look like ribs. (They should be readily available at your grocery store; if you have trouble finding them, ask the people behind the meat counter to help you.) From the loin they are completely boneless, and from the butt they are almost boneless. Either way, you can't go wrong.

2 to 3 pounds country-style spare ribs (about ½ to ¾ pound per person)
¼ cup Dry BBQ Rub (page 195)
1 to 2 cups BBQ Sauce (page 196)

Set the oven to 350 degrees.

Line a baking pan with heavy-duty aluminum foil (this makes cleaning up easier). Put the ribs on the foil and sprinkle the dry rub evenly over them. (Despite its name, *don't* rub it in.) Cover the pan with a tent of heavy-duty aluminum foil; fold over the edges to seal. Bake for 1½ hours, or until very tender.

Near the end of the baking time, preheat a grill or broiler.

Remove the ribs from the oven and then grill or broil them until you are happy.

Heat the BBQ sauce in a saucepan. Spoon or brush some sauce on each portion and serve the ribs with more warm sauce on the side.

Yield: 4 servings

BBQ CHICKEN

We have to believe that everyone who owns even the tiniest hibachi has cooked plenty of BBQ chicken. Some folks like to boil the chicken before grilling, but baking it seems to retain more of the flavor and natural juices. (Plus, you can use the rub). If you have a smoker, a quick hot smoke (about 20 minutes) before grilling is even better.

1 whole chicken (3 to 4 pounds), cut up, or 3 to 4 pounds chicken pieces
¼ to ½ cup Dry BBQ Rub (page 195)
1 to 2 cups BBQ Sauce (see page 196)

Set the oven to 375 degrees.

Put the chicken in a baking pan lined with heavy-duty aluminum foil (this makes cleanup easier). Sprinkle the dry rub on all sides of the chicken. (Despite its name, *don't* rub it in.) Cover the pan with a tent of heavy-duty aluminum foil; fold over the edges to seal. Bake for 45 minutes to an hour.

Travis Hodgkins, "Omelet King and Smoke Daddy," with Josie

Near the end of the baking time, preheat a grill or broiler.

Remove the chicken from the oven, and set aside for 10 to 15 minutes. Then grill or broil it until you are happy. (We like it pretty crispy.)

Heat the BBQ sauce in a saucepan. Spoon some sauce over each piece of chicken and serve the chicken with extra warm sauce on the side.

Yield: 4 to 6 servings

CHAPTER 4

SIDES

We have many customers who are connoisseurs of sides. They make their whole meal out of FGTs (Fried Green Tomatoes) and a big bowl of Mashed Potatoes. Others settle in for Pimiento & Cheese sandwiches and Summer Salad. On BBQ nights—feast time for carnivores—the vegetarian meal of choice is Black-eyed Pea Succotash, Mashed Potatoes, and Collards. So you can think of sides as dinner in disguise. Some of them—like Hushpuppies and FGTs (which we serve with eggs and toast)—also work for breakfast.

But sides also make great appetizers and accompaniments. Cooking up a side—or a bunch of 'em—makes the meal more interesting and tasty and, in some ways, more surprising to your family or guests. Grilled steak is great, but add some Summer Salad and some Jo-Jos and it's even better. Likewise, a bagel breakfast gets one step tastier (and a little more special) with some Smoked Trout Pâté.

So feel free to go to town making these sides. The only part of the meal they probably won't work for is dessert.

An old photo of River Run when it was Crow's Lunch.

CORN & OYSTER CASSEROLE

When Maya spent her first Christmas in Mississippi, she was amazed at the number of casseroles on the holiday table. This is always one of them. Some Northerners can't seem to acquire the taste for it, but others can't get enough. It's rich and filling, so serve small portions with roast turkey, chicken, or baked ham or, as Jimmy's mom does, as part of a smorgasbord of casseroles.

    4 cups crushed saltines (about 90 crackers, or ½ box)
    2 pounds canned creamed corn
    1 pound fresh or canned shucked oysters
    Salt, to taste
    Freshly ground black pepper, to taste
    4 tablespoons (½ stick) unsalted butter, cut into small pieces

Set the oven to 350 degrees.

In a 1½-quart casserole dish that is about 4 inches deep, sprinkle some of the crumbled saltines—just enough to cover the bottom. Then, ever so gently, spoon or pour some of the corn over the crackers, just enough to cover. Next, place the oysters an inch or so apart on top of the corn. (If the oysters are really big, cut them into chunks.) Sprinkle with salt and pepper. Repeat this layering process until you reach the top of the dish, making sure you finish with cracker crumbs. (You may have a tiny bit of creamed corn left over.) Dot with butter.

Bake until the top is browned and the sides are bubbling a little, 35 to 45 minutes. (A glass dish will take the longer cooking time.)

Yield: 8 to 10 servings

Josie James Kennedy.

CORN BREAD DRESSING

This is especially good with grilled pork chops, which, if you are a Yankee, you will eat with applesauce, but, if you are a Southerner, you will eat with ketchup. Also good with roast chicken, turkey, or ham.

4 cups crumbled Corn Bread (page 60)
1 medium onion, peeled and chopped (about 1 cup)
1 small stalk celery, trimmed and chopped (about ½ cup)
2 eggs, beaten
1 cup chicken or turkey stock or canned broth
8 tablespoons (1 stick) unsalted butter, melted
1 cup finely chopped fresh parsley
2 tablespoons finely chopped fresh sage, or 1 tablespoon dried
Salt, to taste
Freshly ground black pepper, to taste

Set the oven to 400 degrees.

In a large bowl, mix all the ingredients, stirring until everything is blended together well. In a shallow casserole dish (an 8-by-8-inch square pan works well), spread the dressing and bake, uncovered, for 30 minutes, or until it firms up.

Yield: 6 servings

HUSHPUPPIES

Hushpuppies are a given with fried catfish but are just as delicious as a side with other dishes or just by themselves. They make great treats for kids and are the perfect vehicle for ketchup—even better than fries.

Supposedly the name comes from the time when cowboys sat around the campfire at night and threw scraps from the pot to the dogs to keep them from barking.

4 cups yellow cornmeal
2 cups all-purpose flour
1 teaspoon baking powder
1 teaspoon baking soda
2 teaspoons salt
1 teaspoon freshly ground black pepper
3 eggs
3 cups buttermilk
4 green onions, trimmed and chopped
Canola oil, for frying (about 10 cups for a 4-quart Dutch oven)

Mix the cornmeal, flour, baking powder, baking soda, salt, and pepper in a large bowl. In a separate bowl, blend the eggs and buttermilk and add them to the dry ingredients. Add the green onions and mix well.

Set the oven to warm. Line a baking sheet with a brown paper bag or paper towels.

Heat 2 to 3 inches of oil in a Dutch oven until it reaches 325 degrees on a deep-fry thermometer. Grease a metal soup spoon or tablespoon by sticking

144

it in the hot oil, then dip it into the batter. Drop several spoonfuls of the batter—one at a time—into the oil and fry until brown and floating in the oil; this should take about 3 or 4 minutes. Don't crowd the pan. Remove the cooked hushpuppies from the oil with tongs or a slotted spoon and set them on the lined baking sheet to drain. Keep them warm in the oven while you finish frying up the rest of the batter. Grease the spoon as needed and be sure to keep an eye on the temperature of the oil; try to keep it steady, between 325 and 350 degrees.

Serve ASAP.

Yield: about 2 dozen, or 6 to 8 servings

Jimmy with Nadine and Ruby

FRIED GREEN TOMATOES

FGTs are probably the most asked-for weekend breakfast special. Larry Mires, one of our most faithful customers, recently announced that Fried Green Tomatoes and poached eggs make for the best breakfast anyone could possibly eat. They're also great as a side with lunch or dinner or as a vegetarian entrée.

Larry Mires, nonprofit administrator; Rebecca Davison, freelance editor and writer; and Basho

4 or 5 large green tomatoes
2 cups buttermilk
2 cups yellow cornmeal
1 cup all-purpose flour
2 teaspoons salt
1 teaspoon freshly ground black
    pepper
1 teaspoon garlic powder
½ teaspoon cayenne pepper
    (optional, but really good)
Canola oil, for frying (⅔ to 1½ cups
    for a 10-inch skillet)

Rinse the tomatoes and slice them ¼ inch to ⅜ inch thick, just a little thicker than you would slice a red tomato for a sandwich. Soak the slices in the buttermilk for a few minutes. (Sometimes we let them soak overnight, but it's not really necessary.)

Set the oven to warm. Line a baking sheet with a brown paper bag or paper towels.

In a bowl, mix the cornmeal, flour, salt, black pepper, garlic powder, and cayenne (if using).

In a heavy skillet, heat ¼ to ½ inch of oil until quite hot; the surface should look wavy.

While the oil is heating, take the tomatoes out of the buttermilk and dredge them in the cornmeal mixture, patting it on with your hands to coat well. Gently drop the coated tomatoes into the hot skillet—don't crowd the pan—and fry on both sides until golden brown, about 2 to 3 minutes per side. Remove from the oil and place on the prepared baking sheet to drain. Keep them warm in the oven while you continue frying all the tomatoes.

Yield: about 8 servings (2 or 3 slices per serving)

FRIED DILL PICKLES

Most dairy bars, convenience stores, and mom & pop restaurants in the South serve fried dill pickles. The old A-Frame Dairy Bar in Shannon, Mississippi, was Jimmy's favorite place to get them, along with a sliced steak sandwich deluxe. Some places slice the pickle crosswise, very thin, and some quarter them. We like to slice them on the diagonal, the size of a potato chip. And as they say about certain potato chips, "Bet you can't eat just one."

    1 cup buttermilk
    2 eggs
    2 cups all-purpose flour
    Salt, to taste
    Freshly ground black pepper, to taste
    Canola oil, for frying (about 10 cups for a 4-quart Dutch oven)
    4 large kosher dill pickles, sliced thin on the diagonal

Mix the buttermilk and eggs together in one bowl, and the flour, salt, and pepper in another.

Heat 2 to 3 inches of oil in a Dutch oven until it reaches 325 to 350 degrees on a deep-fry thermometer.

Line a baking sheet with a brown paper bag or paper towels.

Dip the pickle slices in the buttermilk mixture and then into the seasoned flour. Using tongs, drop the coated pickles, one by one, into the hot oil; fry about 2 pickles' worth of slices in each batch. Be sure to regulate the heat so that the oil stays between 325 and 350 degrees.

When the pickles are a light golden color (this should take 7 to 9 minutes), remove them with tongs or a slotted spoon and drain them on the prepared baking sheet. Repeat with the remaining pickles.

Sprinkle a little salt on them (remember, pickles are pretty salty) and serve as you would French fries.

Yield: 6 to 8 servings

Bryna Levin, television producer.

NEUROTIC SALAD

Maya's close friend Bryna Levin gave us this recipe. She calls it "Neurotic Salad" because of the somewhat nitpicky instructions to cut all the ingredients into the size of a corn kernel. This can be time-consuming but oddly relaxing, especially if you are working at the porch table in the summer. And summer is the time to make this salad—the taste depends heavily on fresh, ripe ingredients.

2 large ears fresh corn, husked
1 small zucchini
2 ripe tomatoes
½ red onion
3 tablespoons olive oil

2 tablespoons lime juice
Salt, to taste
Freshly ground black pepper, to taste
⅓ cup chopped fresh cilantro

Steam or boil the corn a few minutes. Allow to cool. When cool enough to handle, cut a straight slice off the fat end of each ear. Stand an ear on this flat end in a shallow bowl and, using a sharp knife, cut the kernels off. Do the same with the other ear. You should have 2 cups.

Cut the zucchini lengthwise into 4 wedges. Cut the seeds off, leaving only ½ inch of flesh next to the skin. Discard the seeds. Cut each wedge into 3 or 4 strips, then dice into pieces the size of a corn kernel.

Stem the tomatoes and cut them in half. Scoop out the seeds with a teaspoon. Cut the flesh into kernel-sized pieces.

Peel the red onion and dice it into kernel-sized pieces.

In a small bowl, whisk together the oil and lime juice. Season with salt and pepper. Whisk in the cilantro. Toss with the vegetables.

Allow the salad to sit for a while for the flavors to blend. Serve at room temperature with grilled chicken, burgers, or chops.

Yield: about 4 servings

SUMMER SALAD

This is another recipe that brings back lots of memories for Jimmy. His mom made this vegetable-and-vinegar combo all summer long, and it made its appearance everywhere, from lunch boxes to catfish dinners. Maya makes it a lot now, too, although she sometimes uses balsamic vinegar, and a little less sugar than Mom did.

> 1 medium cucumber, chopped (about 1½ cups)
> 1 medium tomato, chopped (about 1 cup)
> ½ small red onion, peeled and chopped (about ½ cup)
> ¼ cup minced fresh parsley
> ½ cup white vinegar
> 2 tablespoons sugar
> 1 cup water

Put all the ingredients in a bowl and stir. You may want to add more water or sugar to taste.

Serve in individual bowls and eat with a spoon.

Yield: about 4 servings

MAYA'S SLAW

Crunchy and fresh—dress this right at the last minute. Great as a topping for Pulled Pork (page 134) or as a side with any BBQ.

For the dressing:
¼ cup red wine vinegar
¼ cup cider vinegar
¼ cup mayonnaise
1½ teaspoons prepared Dijon mustard
½ cup vegetable oil
1½ teaspoons sugar
2 teaspoons salt
1 teaspoon freshly ground black pepper

For the slaw:
½ head red cabbage
½ head green cabbage
1 red bell pepper, seeded and thinly sliced
½ medium red onion, peeled and thinly sliced
½ cup chopped fresh cilantro or parsley

Maya Kennedy.

In a medium bowl, whisk together the dressing ingredients. Cover and refrigerate until ready to serve. This will keep 3 or 4 days, covered, in the refrigerator.

Remove and discard the tough outer leaves from both heads of cabbage. Core the cabbages. Shred them in a food processor or with a sharp knife.

In a large salad bowl, toss the slaw ingredients together. Right before serving, toss the slaw with the dressing.

Yield: 6 to 8 servings

A PAGE FROM THE TOWN CONSTABLE'S LOG
PLAINFIELD, VERMONT

4/8 5 P.M. Serve search warrant for dog "Bubba" at residence of Duane Drysdale. Dog to pound.

1 P.M.: Rec. call from Betty Caruso, live animal in feedbag on Lower Road. Investigate. Long-haired black cat in bag. Escapes into woods. Notify neighbors.

2 P.M.: Rec. call from Elvira Longhorn, sheep-killer dog in her yard. Investigate. Not seen.

2:30: Returning to Village, note border collie dog loose, chasing cars on road. No tags. Belongs to G. Sheperd, gray trailer up road. Take dog home. No one present. Leave warning note.

3 P.M.: Call from Elvira Longhorn about dog above chasing her vehicle. Told her not the sheep-killer.

4/11 11:30 P.M.: Return search warrant as served to Superior Court, Barre. Call to Town Clerk, Bubba now vaccinated and registered.

5/20 10 A.M.: T/C at work from Frank McNamara. Attack rooster bothering his children. Rooster is tattered and torn.
   12:45 P.M.: To area, find rooster and terminate him. Report same to McNamara.

7/9—Call from Beebe's Farm Stand. Strange dog afraid of lightning and thunder, taken refuge and won't leave. This is E. Montpelier, I call that Constable—James Caruthers—his phone out. Go to Beebe's, they really want the dog gone. Take dog to general store, E. Mont., to see if anyone recognizes it, no dice. Another call to Caruthers. Leave message. Take dog to pound.

7/10—Call from Caruthers, notify him of story.

7/29 T/C Mrs. Brannon, raccoon wandering around her mother-in-law's yard. Go there, been gone for 15 minutes. Return home, call from Mrs. Brannon, Mr. Borden (?) has hoed porcupine to death in his yard. I dispose of same.

9/5 Call from East Hill at 7 A.M. Wild cat in house. To house, capture cat, take to pound. 19 miles, 1 hour.

This page was taken exactly from the log of Town Constable Rick Levy. The names of the residents and their animals were changed to protect both the innocent and the not-so-innocent.

JO-JOS

Jo-Jos are nothing more than a deep-fried potato wedge, like a big ol' French fry that's been coated with batter. Not only are Jo-Jos the best things that have ever spent time under a convenience store heat lamp, but they also have a great name.

        4 large white potatoes
        1 cup buttermilk
        2 cups all-purpose flour
        1 tablespoon salt, plus more for sprinkling
        1 tablespoon coarsely ground black pepper
        1½ teaspoons garlic powder
        Canola oil, for frying (about 10 cups for a 4-quart Dutch oven)

Line a baking sheet with a brown paper bag or paper towels.

Scrub the potatoes but don't peel them. Cut each lengthwise into 8 wedges. Soak the wedges briefly (a few minutes will do it) in the buttermilk.

Combine the flour, salt, pepper, and garlic powder in a shallow dish and stir. Roll each soaked potato wedge in the seasoned flour, patting the flour on with your fingers so the potatoes are really coated.

Meanwhile, heat 2 to 3 inches of oil in a Dutch oven until it reaches 325 to 350 degrees on a deep-fry thermometer. Drop in some of the potatoes (work in batches, frying one potato's worth, or 8 wedges, at a time). Cook for about 7 minutes; they will still be quite pale. Be sure to keep an eye on the temperature of the oil while you work, and regulate the heat to keep it steady, between 325 and 350 degrees. Remove the potato wedges to the lined baking sheet and let them rest for a few minutes or several hours. Repeat with remaining potato wedges. (You can do this the night before you are serving; cover and refrigerate the partially done potatoes, but bring them to room temperature before refrying.)

Just before serving, bring the oil back to between 325 and 350 degrees and fry the wedges again, another 7 or 8 minutes. The Jo-Jos should be dark golden brown. To test for doneness, cut one open and taste; make sure it is tender inside and crispy on the outside.

Sprinkle with a bit of salt, if desired, and serve.

Note: If you are in a hurry, you can fry the Jo-Jos in one step—it will still take about 15 minutes total. But, like classic French fries, they are much better when they are partially fried, left to rest, and then fried again.

Yield: about 8 servings

MASHED POTATOES

These are good, basic mashed potatoes. If you want to fancy them up a bit, add roasted garlic, fresh herbs, or spices.

     5 pounds potatoes
     8 tablespoons (1 stick) unsalted butter
     1 cup half-and-half
     2 teaspoons salt
     1 teaspoon freshly ground black pepper

We don't peel the potatoes, but you can if you want to. If leaving the peels on, scrub them and cut out any imperfections. Cut them into chunks.

Put the potatoes in a large pot and add enough cold water to cover. Bring to a boil and cook until really soft.

Drain the potatoes and return them to the pot or put them in a big bowl. While they are still hot, mash them with a potato masher. Add the butter, a bit at a time, and keep mashing until it is well incorporated. Add the half-and-half, salt, and pepper and keep mashing until the potatoes are as smooth as you like. (We like them lumpy.) Taste and add more salt, and pepper if needed.

Serve immediately, preferably with plenty of gravy.

Yield: 6 to 8 servings

SHAKEN POTATOES

This is Maya's favorite way to make and eat potatoes. It's also her recipe.

6 medium-large red potatoes, cut into 6 or 8 chunks each, or
    36 tiny new potatoes
4 tablespoons (½ stick) unsalted butter, cut into a few chunks
⅓ cup chopped fresh parsley
Salt, to taste
Freshly ground black pepper, to taste

Put the potatoes in a pot with a handles and a lid. Cover them with water, put the lid on, and bring them to a boil. Reduce the heat and simmer until the potatoes are tender. Drain them in a colander. While still piping hot, return them to the pot they were cooked in.

Add the butter, parsley, and a little salt and pepper. Cover the pot with the lid and, using hot pads, grab the handles and the lid at the same time and shake the pot vigorously up and down and all around. Check to make sure everything is mixed up well and shake again, if needed.

Taste for salt and pepper and serve.

Yield: 4 to 6 servings

POTATO SALAD

This recipe is an attempt to duplicate the mashed potato salad served at TKE's, a drugstore and soda fountain that operated in Tupelo, Mississippi, when Jimmy was growing up. TKE's has since closed, but somehow the potato salad made its way over to a Tupelo restaurant called Finney's. They closely guard their recipe, but this is close.

  2½ pounds red potatoes
  2½ pounds white potatoes
  2 green bell peppers, seeded and chopped fine (about 2 cups)
  One 4-ounce jar pimientos, drained
  1 medium onion, peeled and chopped fine (about 1 cup)
  2 to 2½ cups mayonnaise (according to your taste)
  1 teaspoon cayenne pepper
  1 teaspoon paprika
  2 tablespoons prepared yellow mustard
  2 tablespoons salt
  1 teaspoon freshly ground black pepper
  Dash hot sauce

 We don't peel the potatoes, but you can if you like. If you are not peeling them, scrub them and remove any imperfections.

 Cut the potatoes into bite-sized chunks. Put them in a large pot, cover them with cold water, cover the pot, and bring the water to a boil. Reduce the heat to a low boil and cook until tender.

While the potatoes are cooking, combine the rest of the ingredients in a large bowl. When the potatoes are done, drain them and let them cool slightly (they should still be warm), then mix them with the stuff in the bowl. We like to use a potato masher to make the salad nice and smooth, TKE style. If you like your potato salad chunkier, just use a big spoon to toss the potatoes with the other ingredients.

Serve slightly warm or at room temperature.

Yield: 10 to 12 servings

PIMIENTO & CHEESE

Reynolds Price, a novelist and native of Macon, North Carolina, calls this spread "the peanut butter of my childhood." It was the peanut butter of Jimmy's childhood too. As with peanut butter, tastes vary: Jimmy likes his Pimiento & Cheese spread kind of regular on white bread; his brother, Joseph, piles it on about 2 inches thick; Maya likes it on Jules Rabin's sourdough French; Price recommends "rough brown bread"; and Marialisa adds sliced tomatoes and onions. At any rate, one of the first things Jimmy does when he goes home to Mississippi is to make a stack of Pimiento & Cheese sandwiches to go along with a big ol' plate of fried chicken and a glass of very strong, unsweetened iced tea.

Antha Williams, waitress. "This job is great.... I can be surly and still make money."

4 cups grated cheddar cheese
1 cup mayonnaise
One 4-ounce jar chopped pimientos, drained
¼ teaspoon sugar
¼ teaspoon salt
¼ teaspoon freshly ground black pepper

    Mix all the ingredients in a large bowl until pretty well blended.

    Yield: about 4 cups of spread, enough for at least 8 sandwiches, unless you're Jimmy's brother.

(Recipe reprinted from *The Great American Writers' Cookbook*; Dean Faulkner, editor. Courtesy Yoknapatawpha Press.)

164

SMOKED TROUT PÂTÉ

We used to make this pâté—with Maya's mom's help—and sell it under the "Three Little Fish Co." label. We're no longer in the pâté business, but we still make this spread as a weekend special. It's great on bagels or sourdough French, with sliced red onions and lemon wedges served on the side.

8 ounces smoked trout
6 ounces cream cheese (about ¾ cup), at room temperature
¼ cup half-and-half
1 green onion, trimmed and chopped
1 teaspoon prepared mustard, preferably Dijon
1 tablespoon freshly squeezed lemon juice
½ teaspoon dried dill
¼ teaspoon freshly ground black pepper

Place the trout in the bowl of a food processor and blend until completely broken down into small pieces. Remove the trout from the processor and set it aside. Add all of the remaining ingredients to the processor and blend until well mixed. Stop the processor and scrape the sides with a rubber spatula once or twice so that everything is mixed well. Add the trout to the mixture, a little bit at a time, until it is mixed in.

Scrape the pâté out into a bowl, cover, and refrigerate until well chilled—overnight is good. When you are ready to serve the pâté, scoop a dollop onto a serving plate with an ice cream scoop or large spoon.

Yield: 2 cups, or at least 8 servings

BLACK-EYED PEA SUCCOTASH

Another recipe from chef Josh Grinker. A good side dish for breakfast, lunch, or dinner.

½ pound dried black-eyed peas (to make about 3 cups cooked)
1 chicken bouillon cube
¾ pound thick-cut bacon, cubed
1 small onion, peeled and chopped (about ¾ cup)
2 tablespoons total chopped fresh herbs (thyme, oregano, and/or
    basil), or 2 teaspoons dried
1 tablespoon minced garlic
½ pound frozen corn kernels, thawed and drained (about 1¾ cups)
1 medium tomato, cored and chopped (about 1 cup)
2 tablespoons chicken broth
¼ cup heavy cream
Salt, to taste
Freshly ground black pepper, to taste

The night before you are going to make the succotash, rinse the black-eyed peas and pick them over, discarding any small stones or funny-looking peas. Soak the peas overnight in enough cold water to cover by several inches.

The next morning, drain the peas. Return them to the pot, cover them with several inches of water again, add the bouillon cube, and bring the pot to a

Ben Koenig, owner of the Country Bookshop, across the road from River Run.

boil. Reduce to a simmer and cook until the peas are tender (this usually takes about an hour, but the time depends on the age of the peas). Set aside.

If you have forgotten to soak the peas overnight or don't have the time, use the quick-soak method: Prepare the peas as above, but instead of soaking them overnight, bring them to a boil. Boil for 2 minutes, shut off the heat, and let the peas sit for about an hour. Drain them and proceed to cook as above.

Most of the water should be absorbed when the peas are done. Drain off any extra and set the peas aside.

Line a plate with paper towels.

In a heavy skillet, fry the bacon until just crisp. Remove from the skillet with a slotted spoon and set aside on the lined plate to drain.

Drain off all but 1 to 2 tablespoons of the bacon grease, add the onion to the skillet, and set over medium heat. Add the herbs and garlic and sauté, stirring, until the onion and garlic are soft, 7 to 10 minutes.

Add the corn to the skillet, along with the cooked black-eyed peas, cooked bacon, and chopped tomato; cook, stirring, a few minutes over medium-low heat. Add the broth and cream and stir. Taste and season with salt and pepper, as needed.

Cook until just heated through and serve.

Yield: 8 servings

COLLARDS (COOKED GREENS)

The first thing we think of when we hear the word "collards" is the distinctive smell of the kitchen when they are being cooked. It's a good smell, one that reminds us of home and the good eating that is to come. A natural with Pulled Pork (page 134), BBQ Chicken (page 137), or Country-Style Spare Ribs (page 136).

> 3 or 4 bunches collards, mustard greens, turnip greens, or chard (3 to 4 pounds total)
> 1 medium onion, peeled and chopped (about 1 cup)
> 1 to 2 tablespoons minced garlic
> Ham hock or, for vegetarians, ¼ cup powdered vegetable soup base
> Hot pepper vinegar, for serving

Trim, roughly chop, rinse, and drain the greens. Put them in a very large pot with the onion, garlic, and ham hock (or vegetable base). Cover with cold water by several inches. Bring to a boil, then reduce the heat and let simmer for 1 week. (Just kidding—but it does take a good part of the day for them to get cooked and tender, maybe 6 to 8 hours.)

Drain and serve hot with hot pepper vinegar on the side.

Yield: 8 to 10 servings

CHAPTER 5

SAUCES, GRAVIES, MARINADES & SALAD DRESSINGS

An old photo of the Plainfield post office in the River Run building.

These recipes provide the finishing touches to a lot of our dishes. We use several of them daily at River Run and as many as half of them on most weekends.

Gravy making seems to have become something of a lost art, and we think you'll be surprised at how easily these gravies whip up and how much your family and friends appreciate them. There's been a lot written recently about "comfort food," and gravy has got to be a prime example.

We've given you ideas about how we use each recipe, but there is no limit to what your imagination might suggest. In fact, you may want to make some of the sauces and marinades in double batches to use later in the week or to freeze for the more distant future. It can be daunting to think about making a sauce or marinade for a dish you want to eat right away, but if you have some made up in advance, you're in for almost instant gratification.

Because of the versatility of all these sauces, gravies, marinades, and dressings, we hope this chapter becomes a well-worn section of the book.

170

HOT PEPPER HOLLANDAISE

There are many variations on blender Hollandaise but—with or without the jalapeño—this is a never-fail version that we use all the time. It is especially good on Grit Cakes (page 43) and Omelets (page 75).

8 tablespoons (1 stick) unsalted butter
1 jalapeño pepper, stemmed, seeded and chopped (see note)
6 egg yolks
1 teaspoon freshly squeezed lemon juice or cider vinegar
1 teaspoon white pepper
1 teaspoon dry mustard
1 teaspoon salt

Melt the butter in a saucepan and keep over very low heat.
    Put the jalapeño, egg yolks, lemon juice (or vinegar), white pepper, mustard, and salt in a blender or food processor and pulse until blended.

Return the butter to high heat and, when very hot but not burning—quickly, before the butter cools!—add it to the blender or food processor with the motor running. It will thicken slightly but will still be fairly runny.

Use immediately or cover and refrigerate until ready to use, but no longer than a few hours.

Note: You can substitute red bell pepper or sun-dried tomatoes for the japaleño if you wish.

Yield: about 1 cup

CHEESE SAUCE

We use this sauce on Omelets (page 75) and other eggs, Biscuits (page 64), and Grit Cakes (page 43). You can also mix it with noodles for homemade mac & cheese.

1 cup (2 sticks) unsalted butter
1 cup all-purpose flour
2 cups half-and-half or whole milk
2 cups (8 ounces) grated cheddar cheese (see note)

2 tablespoons (total) chopped fresh herbs; parsley, basil, oregano, or whatever you have on hand
Salt, to taste
Freshly grated black pepper, to taste

Melt the butter in a heavy-bottomed pot or Dutch oven over medium heat and stir in the flour with a whisk until it is well blended. Continue stirring, letting it cook for a minute or two. Add the half-and-half (or milk) and keep whisking for another couple of minutes.

Add the cheese and stir with whisk until it melts and is blended into the mixture. Adjust the heat to low. Add the herbs, salt, and pepper and cook while stirring for 3 or 4 more minutes. Do not overcook, or the sauce will toughen and form a ball.

This is best used the day it is made but can be kept, covered and refrigerated, for 2 or 3 days.

Note: You can use any cheese for this sauce, but if it's a stronger-flavored one, like blue or chèvre, use only 1 cup.

Yield: about 4 cups

173

TARTAR SAUCE

If you're frying fish or seafood, you're going to need tartar sauce. This recipe takes very little effort and is way better than the kind you buy in a jar.

Robert Voorhees, sailor.

1½ cups mayonnaise
¼ medium onion, peeled and minced (about ¼ cup)
¼ cup minced dill pickle
2 tablespoons lemon juice
2 tablespoons minced fresh parsley
1 tablespoon prepared Dijon or yellow mustard
½ teaspoon Old Bay seasoning
½ teaspoon white pepper
¼ teaspoon cayenne pepper
Salt, to taste
Freshly ground black pepper, to taste

Mix everything together in a bowl or jar. Cover and refrigerate until ready to use, up to 3 or 4 days.
Yield: about 2 cups

174

CRAWFISH CREOLE SAUCE

This is another sauce that is great on just about everything. We serve it mostly on open-faced Biscuits (page 64), eggs, Grit Cakes (page 43), and pasta. It feeds eight to ten; consider halving the recipe if cooking for a smaller crowd.

¼ cup canola oil
2 medium onions, peeled and chopped (about 2 cups)
1 tablespoon minced garlic
1½ green bell peppers, seeded and chopped (about 1½ cups)
2 small stalks celery, trimmed and chopped (about 1 cup)
One 28-ounce can crushed tomatoes
1 tablespoon salt
1 teaspoon cayenne pepper
1 teaspoon white pepper
1 teaspoon freshly ground black pepper
1½ teaspoons dried thyme
½ teaspoon dried basil
½ teaspoon dried oregano
2 pounds crawfish meat or shrimp (50/60 count)

Heat the oil in a heavy-bottomed pan or Dutch oven set over medium heat. Sauté the onions, garlic, bell peppers, and celery until soft, 7 to 10 minutes.

Add the tomatoes, seasonings, and herbs and cook at a simmer, with the pot mostly covered, for 30 minutes.

If you are using crawfish meat, it is probably precooked, so add it and cook just enough to warm it through. If using shrimp, shell it and add it to the pot; cook until just done, 3 to 5 minutes (do not overcook). The sauce will keep for 2 or 3 days, covered, in the refrigerator. Reheat before serving.

Yield: about 10 cups, or 8 to 10 servings

Kevin Rand, a local contractor, was the volunteer foreman in charge when 50 or so volunteers showed up on each of two jammed weekends to rebuild Tim and Sarah Coldings's barn after it burned down.

RANCHERO SAUCE

Chunky and tasty, this sauce gives Huevos Rancheros (recipe below) its name, and it's just as good on home fries, Corn Fritters (page 39), or even toast or pasta. Use your imagination.

> Two 28-ounce cans whole tomatoes, drained and chopped, juice
>   reserved
> 1 medium onion, peeled and chopped (about 1 cup)
> 1 green bell pepper, seeded and chopped (about 1 cup)
> 4 cloves garlic, peeled and minced
> 2 teaspoons salt
> 2 teaspoons ground cumin
> 1 teaspoon chili powder
> ½ to 1 teaspoon cayenne pepper
> 1 teaspoon white pepper
> 1 teaspoon freshly ground black pepper
> 2 jalapeño or serrano chili peppers, stemmed, seeded and chopped
>   (optional)

Mix all ingredients in a stainless-steel saucepan or other nonreactive pan. This sauce is plenty spicy without the optional chili peppers, but if you want the sauce hotter, go for it. If you plan to cook the sauce for a long time—say, 3 to 4 hours—which is how we like to do it, put in all the reserved tomato juice. If you only have an hour (it'll still be good), put in just a little bit of the juice.

Cook over low heat, at just a bare simmer, for 1 to 4 hours, with the pot mostly covered. You can make the sauce 2 to 3 days ahead of time and re-frigerate it until just before serving. Serve hot. You can also freeze it up to 3 months.

Huevos Rancheros: Warm a flour tortilla, a biscuit (page 64), or a fried or broiled grit cake (page 43). Top it with eggs done to your liking (scrambled, fried, etc.). Pour Ranchero Sauce over all.

   Yield: 3 to 4 cups, or 6 to 8 servings

Mill workers.

PLAINFIELD, VERMONT

"You're so lucky to live here," the visitors invariably say. Then there's a pause and a clearing of throats. "But what do you *do?*"

One hundred years ago, no one would even have thought to ask. One hundred years ago a remarkable number of businesses were flourishing in Plainfield: at least two sawmills, a creamery, a huge hotel, a bobbin factory, a machine shop, a cheese factory, a brickyard, a cooper, a slaughterhouse, and many retail markets, taverns, grocery stores, and blacksmith shops, not to mention numerous hillside farms. The town was alive with the doings of the local theater company, two community bands, the Independent Order of Oddfellows, the Modern Woodmen, the Sons and Daughters of Liberty, the

Grange, and the Mother's Club. Plainfield even boasted a spa, built near the sulfurous waters of a nearby stream. A town history compares The Spring House—favorably, of course—to Saratoga Springs.

Plainfield's a lot quieter nowadays. The railroad—which brought prosperity and growth in 1867—is gone, and the automobile and resulting road construction made it ever more possible to live in one place and work in another, drawing locals to jobs in the nearby cities of Barre (famous for its granite quarries) and Montpelier (the state capital).

But Plainfield is still a community with a personality and a soul. There are still a few small farms clinging to the rocky hillside. Old lefties—holdovers from Goddard College's heyday in the sixties and seventies—make their living as writers, artisans, and environmentalists. A few small businesses—the Winooksi Valley Co-op (natural foods), The Country Bookshop (used books), the Blinking Light Gallery (crafts and artwork), the hardware store, a new pizzeria, and various antique and used furniture shops—are thriving. Goddard itself, founded in 1938 as "A School for Vermont Living," still attracts a lively, if small, student body.

At some point, everyone in town comes together. It might be for Old Home Week or a contra dance at Town Hall. Often it's for morning coffee at River Run.

MARINARA SAUCE

This recipe—a mix of tomatoes and a few seasonings—proves that sometimes the simplest dishes are the best. This sauce turns out surprisingly spicy; it's great plain but even better with mussels (see recipe below). This recipe could easily be halved, but a better idea is to cook the whole recipe and freeze half.

2 tablespoons olive oil
1 large or 2 medium onions, peeled and chopped (1½ to 2 cups)
4 teaspoons minced garlic
One #10 can (6 pounds 6 ounces), or four 28-ounce cans good-quality
   tomatoes, with juice
2 tablespoons chopped fresh basil, or 4 teaspoons dried
1 tablespoon salt
1 tablespoon coarsely ground black pepper
1 teaspoon white pepper
1½ teaspoons sugar
½ teaspoon ground nutmeg

Heat the oil in a large, heavy-bottomed pot or Dutch oven set over medium heat. Sauté the onion until soft, 7 to 10 minutes. Add the garlic and cook for another minute or two. Add the tomatoes and stir well, chopping them with your spoon as you stir. Add all the remaining ingredients and simmer over low heat, with the pot mostly covered, for at least an hour.

Keep, covered, in the refrigerator for 3 to 4 days or, well packaged, in the freezer for up to 3 months.

Yield: about 10 cups, or plenty for 2 pounds of pasta, about 6 to 8 servings

Mussels Marinara: Beard about 4 pounds of mussels and run them under cold water. Discard any that do not stay closed. Add them to the sauce just before serving. Cover the pot and cook the mussels until they are all open, 8 to 10 minutes. Discard any mussels that do not open. Serve alone or over pasta.

   Yield: serves 4 if served alone, 6–8 if served with pasta

Peter "TWA" Mercer. "Great coffee, great breakfast. Man, I love this place."

PIZZA SAUCE

This is a rather large recipe, but it can be used many different ways: on pizza or Pizzettas (page 88), of course, but also on pasta, on eggs, or to jazz up some soup. If you want a smaller amount, you can halve the recipe, or make the whole batch and freeze half.

    2 to 3 tablespoons olive oil
    1 medium onion, peeled and chopped (about 1 cup)
    1 large carrot, peeled and chopped (about 1 cup)
    1 tablespoon minced garlic
    One #10 can (6 pounds 6 ounces) or four 28-ounce cans good-quality
        tomatoes, with juice
    1 tablespoon dried basil
    Salt, to taste
    Freshly ground black pepper, to taste
    1 tablespoon dried oregano
    1½ teaspoons dried thyme
    1 cup dry red wine

Heat the oil in a large, heavy-bottomed pot or Dutch oven set over medium heat. Sauté the onion and carrot until they start of soften, 5 to 7 minutes. (The carrot will still be a little crunchy.) Add the garlic and cook for another minute or two. Add the tomatoes (and juice) and simmer, uncovered, for an hour or so. Add the basil, salt, and pepper.

Allow the mixture to cool a bit. Working in batches, process it in a food processor or blender until quite smooth. Return it to the pot and add the oregano, thyme, and wine; simmer, uncovered, for about 30 minutes more.

Keep, covered, in the refrigerator for 3 to 4 days or, well packaged, in the freezer for up to 3 months.

Yield: 8 to 10 cups

Phil Hagopian, artist.

ANCHOVY-CAPER PASTA SAUCE

This recipe is from the South...of Italy. It's a classic puttanesca recipe that Marialisa gave us, knowing that its rich, funky flavors are the kind that fans of River Run appreciate. Our friend and fellow chef Steve Bogart doesn't wait for the pasta—he eats it right out of the pot.

¼ cup olive oil
4 cloves garlic, peeled and minced
One 2-ounce can oil-packed anchovy fillets, drained and chopped
½ teaspoon red pepper flakes, or to taste
One 28-ounce can whole or crushed tomatoes, with juice
¼ cup drained capers
¾ cup pitted and chopped Kalamata or Gaeta olives
Dried or fresh oregano, to taste
Chopped fresh parsley, to taste (optional)

In a heavy-bottomed pot or Dutch oven, heat the oil over medium heat. Add the garlic. Cook briefly, stirring, until softened but not browned, 3 to 5 minutes. Add the anchovies and pepper flakes, mashing the anchovies a bit with a wooden spoon. Cook a few minutes more. (The anchovies will sort of dissolve.) Add the tomatoes (and juice), capers, olives, and oregano. (If using whole canned tomatoes, chop them up a bit as you stir.) Cook over medium to medium-high heat for 10 minutes, stirring.

You can stop cooking now and add the parsley (if using), then cook just a few minutes more before serving. Or you can cook the sauce for about 45 minutes over low heat, with the pot mostly covered. The extra cooking will thicken the sauce, and the flavors will meld better. If you choose the longer cooking time, add the parsley (if using) about 10 minutes before the sauce is done.

We've never had any left, but you can keep it, covered, in the refrigerator for 2 or 3 days.

Yield: About 1 quart, enough for 1 pound spaghetti or linguine, or about 4 servings

Marialisa Calta with family:
Dirk, Emma, and Hannah Van Susteren.

SAUSAGE GRAVY

This is the gravy we use for "B&G" (Biscuits & Gravy) and Dixie Eggs (recipes below). We used to serve B&G only on weekends. However, based on the demand, we had to start serving it every day we're open. There are three or four dishes that help define River Run, and B&G is certainly one of them. This makes *a lot* of gravy, but B&G is the kind of dish you would tend to make for a crowd. You can halve the recipe, but don't try to freeze it.

1 pound loose pork sausage
6¾ cups half-and-half or whole milk
¾ cup all-purpose flour
2 teaspoons salt
2 teaspoons freshly ground black pepper
1 teaspoon garlic powder

In a heavy-bottomed pot or Dutch oven, brown the sausage over medium heat, stirring and breaking it up as you cook. When browned, drain off all the grease. Pour 6 cups of the half-and-half (or milk) over the sausage and increase the heat to medium-high. Heat until hot, but don't let it boil.

In a small bowl, mix the flour with the remaining ¾ cup half-and-half (or milk) and whisk or stir with a fork until it is smooth (no lumps!). Whisk or stir this mixture into the sausage mixture. Reduce the heat to medium-low and continue stirring until the gravy thickens, 5 to 10 minutes.

Remove from the heat and stir in the seasonings. Serve immediately or let cool, cover, and refrigerate until ready to use, up to 3 or 4 days (reheat before serving).

Yield: 8 to 10 cups, or enough for 10 to 12 servings

Biscuits & Gravy: Make 1 recipe of Biscuits (page 64) and put them in the oven just before you start the gravy. Both should be ready about the same time. To serve, split a hot biscuit in half and top with a generous portion of hot gravy.

Dixie Eggs: Make 1 recipe of Biscuits (page 64) and 1 recipe Collards (page 168) or wilt a couple of pounds of well-rinsed fresh spinach. To serve, split a hot biscuit in half, top with the cooked greens, eggs done as you like them, and a generous portion of hot gravy.

Gary "Gravy" Graves.

Joshua Beaudry, Goddard student: "River Run condiments on everything."

DILL GRAVY

Dill gravy was born out of a need for a vegetarian alternative to Sausage Gravy (page 187), which is much in demand as the topping for B&G (Biscuits & Gravy) and Dixie Eggs. You can also serve it over Grit Cakes (page 43), eggs, potatoes, or anything else you think might need a little gravy. This gravy is very simple to make and is *almost* as good as Sausage Gravy.

2½ cups half-and-half
2 cups vegetable stock or canned broth
½ cup all-purpose flour
1 to 2 tablespoons dried dill, or 2 to 4 tablespoons chopped fresh
1 teaspoon garlic powder
2 teaspoons salt
2 teaspoons freshly ground black pepper

In a heavy-bottomed pot or Dutch oven, mix 2 cups of the half-and-half with the stock (or broth). Heat to almost boiling, then turn the heat down to keep the mixture at a low simmer.

In a small bowl, mix the flour with the remaining ½ cup half-and-half and whisk or stir with a fork until it is smooth (no lumps!). Whisk or stir this mixture into the hot broth mixture. Reduce the heat to medium-low and continue stirring until the gravy thickens, 5 to 10 minutes.

Remove from the heat and stir in the seasonings. Serve immediately or let cool, cover, and refrigerate until ready to use, up to 3 or 4 days. Reheat before serving.

Yield: about 5 cups, or 6 to 8 servings

FLANK STEAK MARINADE

This marinade also works well with venison and other game. For venison you might want to add about ¼ cup juniper berries. It can easily be halved or doubled and can be made three to four days ahead of time and kept, covered, in the refrigerator.

    1 cup canola oil
    1 cup red wine vinegar
    1 cup dry red wine
    2 tablespoons minced garlic
    ½ teaspoon each of any or all of the following: dried basil, dried thyme, dried rosemary, dried parsley, cayenne, black pepper, white pepper

Mix all the ingredients together and pour over the steak. Let marinate, covered and refrigerated, overnight.

Yield: about 3 cups, or enough for 3 to 4 pounds of steak

190

Jim Libby, lawyer.

John Kennedy.

MILE-HIGH MARINADE

Jimmy's youngest brother, John Phillip Kennedy, a corporate pilot, came up with this recipe; hence, the name. He uses it mostly for steaks on the grill, but it's also great on seafood and chicken. Our favorite way to use it at River Run is as a marinade for tuna steaks before we grill them. The recipe can easily be halved or doubled and can be made several days ahead of time and kept, covered, in the refrigerator.

2 cups pineapple juice
1½ cups soy sauce
1 cup light brown sugar
1 teaspoon minced fresh ginger

2 teaspoons olive oil
1 teaspoon coarsely ground black
   pepper
2 cloves garlic, peeled and minced

Put all the ingredients in a large quart jar, cover, and shake; or mix them together in a bowl. This is especially good on steak; let the meat marinate, covered and refrigerated, 3 to 4 hours. If using it on seafood, marinate, covered and refrigerated, about 1 hour.

Yield: 1 quart, or enough for 4 to 5 pounds of meat or fish

191

MARINADE FOR CHICKEN OR VEGETABLES

Store-bought lemonade and o.j. are fine in this recipe, but if you have the time, freshly squeezed is always better. We use the marinade mostly when grilling chicken and veggies, but you could also use it when broiling, baking, or pan-frying. Marinating time is about 1 hour. The recipe can easily be halved or doubled and can be made several days ahead of time and kept, covered, in the refrigerator.

2 cups (1 recipe) Maple Vinaigrette (see page 194)
¼ cup lemonade
¼ cup orange juice
¼ cup minced fresh herbs, such as parsley, basil, cilantro, or whatever you have on hand, in any combination

Mix all the ingredients together well. Allow the chicken and/or vegetables to marinate—chicken should be covered and refrigerated—at least an hour.

Yield: about 3 cups, or enough for 2 to 3 pounds of chicken or vegetables

BUTTERMILK DRESSING

This was the only salad dressing we offered for the first few years we were open, and we found it worked on all salads: greens, fruit, meat, and mixed vegetables. It also makes a great dip for raw vegetables and for French fries.

2 tablespoons chopped or grated onion
⅓ cup mayonnaise
1 teaspoon chopped garlic
1 teaspoon finely chopped fresh dill, or ½ teaspoon dried, or more to taste
¼ teaspoon freshly ground black pepper
¼ cup buttermilk, plus more if needed
Dash of hot sauce

In a jar with a lid, combine all the dressing ingredients. Cover and shake to mix well. If too thick, thin with additional buttermilk. Refrigerate, covered, until ready to use. It will keep 3 to 4 days and gets stronger as it stands.

Yield: about ⅔ cup

Ava Rose Prince.

193

MAPLE VINAIGRETTE

We serve two dressings at River Run. This is one of them. The other is Buttermilk Dressing (page 193). A lot of our customers like a mix of equal parts of each dressing on their salads, and we call the combo "Half and Half." The recipe can be halved, but it will keep at least a week, covered, in the refrigerator.

½ cup maple syrup
½ cup cider vinegar
1 cup canola or olive oil
Salt, to taste
Freshly ground black pepper, to taste

We make this by just putting all the ingredients in a bowl and mixing them up or putting them in a jar, screwing on the lid, and shaking.

Yield: 2 cups

DRY BBQ RUB

Chef Josh Grinker, who used to cook at River Run, developed this rub. It works well on all kinds of foods: pork, chicken, fish, beef, even tofu. This recipe makes enough so you can have some on hand in your spice rack. It's a necessary part of all of our BBQ recipes but also makes a great addition to Meat Loaf (page 101), soup (BBQ Chicken & Rice Soup, page 3), or anything else that needs some spicing up. Keep it in a covered container in a cool, dry place and it will last indefinitely.

6 tablespoons granulated sugar
2 tablespoons light or dark brown sugar
4 tablespoons (¼ cup) salt
4 tablespoons (¼ cup) ground cumin
4 tablespoons (¼ cup) coarsely ground
   black pepper
4 tablespoons (¼ cup) chili powder
8 tablespoons (½ cup) paprika
1 teaspoon cayenne pepper

Mix all the ingredients well. Store in an airtight container.
   Yield: 2 cups

SIMPLY THE BEST ALL-PURPOSE BBQ SAUCE

3 cups ketchup
1 cup cider vinegar
¼ cup Worcestershire sauce
1 tablespoon dry mustard
1½ teaspoons freshly ground
    black pepper
½ teaspoon cayenne pepper

½ teaspoon chili powder
4 cloves garlic, peeled and
    minced
¼ medium onion, peeled and
    finely chopped (¼ cup)
¾ cup water
¾ cup light brown sugar

Mix all the ingredients together in a heavy-bottomed pot and stir until well combined. Cook over medium heat for 10 minutes, stirring occasionally to avoid burning the bottom of the pot. Turn the heat to low and simmer, uncovered, for 1½ hours, stirring every once in a while.

Use immediately or store, covered, in the refrigerator up to 1 week.

Yield: 4 cups

CHAPTER 6

DESSERTS & DRINKS

e've been fortunate enough to have some great bakers working with us.

One is Nicole Graves, who started working at River Run when she was just a sophomore at the local high school. Her dad, Gary Graves, who comes in regularly, told us what a great baker his daughter was, and we told him to send her by. She came—bearing a plate of chocolate-filled Cream Puffs (page 215)—and we hired her on the spot. One of the many great things about Nicole is that she understood immediately that a River Run dessert had to be like the rest of our food: delicious, substantial, and down to earth. Although her name is not on the all the recipes here, she is responsible for many of them.

Nessa Rabin, our beautiful and talented waitress/manager, is the daughter of our local bread makers, Jules and Helen Rabin of Upland Bakers, and was a pastry chef in New York City for many years. She has also contributed to our dessert repertoire. It's been a real bonus having her in the front of the house for a bunch of reasons, especially when we have questions about baking. Among the recipes she can claim are the Extreme Brownie Cookies (page 222) and Apricot Scones (page 68).

We find that a River Run meal often leaves customers with no room for dessert. We sell many of these treats as take-out items, to be enjoyed later in the day when the meal itself is, we hope, a happy memory.

Note: Please refer to the notes on ingredients and equipment at the beginning of this book. Briefly, remember that you don't need to sift the flour unless specifically instructed to do so. Also, while you are welcome to use imported chocolate, a good-quality domestic chocolate, like Baker's, works just fine. As equipment for these recipes, you will need standard cake and loaf pans, a 13-by-9-inch brownie pan, a tube pan, and baking parchment. An instant-read thermometer will enable you to determine when custards are properly cooked. An electric mixer is handy but not strictly necessary.

Jimmy and Maya.

BANANA PUDDING

When we got married, our friends and family all worked together to put on a feast; it included Fried Catfish (page 121), of course, and grilled venison, Hushpuppies (page 144), Maya's Slaw (page 153), and Potato Salad (page 162). When it came to dessert, there was no question: Banana Pudding, our favorite. And boy, did we have Banana Pudding! Jimmy's mom and an assembly line of friends assembled it in large Rubbermaid tubs. That was ten years ago, and people are still talking about it.

4 egg yolks, well beaten
½ cup sugar
3 tablespoons all-purpose flour
Pinch salt
2 cups milk, preferably whole milk
4 tablespoons (½ stick) unsalted butter
1 tablespoon vanilla extract
2 bananas, peeled and sliced into ¼-inch-thick rounds
22 vanilla wafers, such as Nabisco brand Nilla wafers, broken into large
  pieces

In a medium-sized bowl, mix the egg yolks and sugar. Add the flour, salt, and ¼ cup of the milk.

In a saucepan, heat the remaining 1¾ cups milk and the butter until the butter is melted and the mixture is steaming. Remove from the heat and whisk the hot milk mixture into the egg mixture. Return this mixture to the saucepan and bring to a low boil, stirring constantly. Cook, stirring all the while, for several minutes. The custard will thicken and the temperature should read 160 degrees on an instant-read thermometer. Put the hot custard in a bowl and stir in the vanilla. Stir in the banana slices and wafers and eat right away, warm, or cover and refrigerate until chilled.

A little whipped cream when serving is not necessary, but it doesn't hurt.
Yield: about 8 servings

AMALGAMATION CAKE

This is a rich, indulgent cake that Jimmy's mom always makes for Christmas, along with all the other baking she does at that time of year. The recipe has been in her family for generations. A friend of ours calls it "Sliver Cake" because it is so sweet and rich you can eat only very thin pieces. It's surprising how quickly it can disappear, one sliver at a time.

For the cake:
1 pound (4 sticks) unsalted butter, at room temperature
2 cups sugar
1 cup milk, preferably whole milk
1 tablespoon baking powder
3 cups all-purpose flour
¾ teaspoon salt
8 egg whites, well chilled

For the icing:
2 cups sugar
1 tablespoon all-purpose flour
1 pound (4 sticks) unsalted butter
1 cup chopped pecans
1 cup chopped walnuts
1 cup golden raisins
1 cup shredded sweetened coconut
8 egg yolks

Juan Antonio and Julian Soberano.

Set the oven to 350 degrees. Grease and flour three 9-inch round cake pans and set them aside.

Make the cake: In a large mixing bowl, cream the butter and sugar together. Add the milk and baking powder and mix. Mix the flour and salt together and add it to the bowl, about 1 cup at a time, beating well between additions.

Beat the egg whites until quite stiff but not dry. (Well-chilled egg whites whip more easily.) Using a large rubber spatula, fold the egg whites into the batter. Mix well. (A quick session with an electric mixer works perfectly.)

The batter will be thick. Divide it among the 3 prepared pans; it will fill them about ½ inch deep, making fairly thin layers. Arrange the pans in the oven so that they don't touch each other or the oven sides.

Bake 20 to 25 minutes, or until a tester inserted in the center of each comes out clean. Since most ovens hold heat unevenly, it is a good idea to switch the positions of the pans about halfway through.

When the cakes are done, allow them to cool for a few minutes in the pans, then remove from the pans and set on racks to cool completely.

Meanwhile, make the icing: Mix all the ingredients in a large, heavy skillet set over medium heat. Stir gently but constantly so the bottom doesn't stick. Cook about 10 minutes; the icing should be bubbling. Allow it to cool to a little warmer than room temperature.

Frost the thoroughly cooled cake layers with the warm icing (the icing hardens as it cools).

Slice only when thoroughly cool. A thin slice would be great with hot black "New Orleans" or "Creole" coffee (flavored with roasted chicory).

Yield: one 9-inch 3-layer cake, or at least 10 servings

COCA-COLA CAKE

A Southern classic.

For the cake:
2 cups all-purpose flour
2 cups sugar
1 teaspoon baking soda
¼ teaspoon salt
2 eggs
1 teaspoon vanilla extract
½ cup buttermilk
1 cup (2 sticks) unsalted butter
1 cup Coca-Cola
2 tablespoons unsweetened cocoa powder

For the frosting:
½ cup (1 stick) unsalted butter, at room temperature
2 tablespoons unsweetened cocoa powder
Pinch salt
1 pound (about 4 cups) confectioner's sugar
¼ cup Coca-Cola
1 teaspoon vanilla extract
1 cup chopped nuts

Set the oven to 350 degrees. Grease a 13-by-9-inch baking pan and set it aside.

Make the cake: Mix the flour, sugar, baking soda, and salt in a large bowl. In a separate bowl, mix the eggs, vanilla, and buttermilk and add to the flour mixture. Bring the butter, Coke, and cocoa powder to a boil in a saucepan and add to the flour mixture. Mix until everything is well blended. Pour the batter into the prepared pan. Bake for 35 to 45 minutes, or until a tester comes out clean.

Remove the cake from the oven and allow it to cool in the pan on a cake rack.

Meanwhile, make the frosting: Cream together the butter, cocoa powder, salt, and confectioner's sugar, using an electric mixer if you like. Add the Coke and vanilla and mix thoroughly. Stir in the nuts by hand.

Frost the cooled cake and serve from the pan.

Yield: one 13-by-9-inch cake, or about 12 servings

Dan "Moon" Fowler, logging contractor. "If this makes money, I want some of it."

204

WHISKEY CAKE

The recipe comes from Jimmy's Aunt Hazel's sister, Regina Lawson. She used to visit Jimmy's family from Kentucky once or twice a year.

1 pound red candied cherries, cut into pieces
½ pound golden raisins or ½ cup chopped dates
1 pint (2 cups) bourbon, plus more for storing cake
6 eggs, separated
¾ pound (3 sticks) unsalted butter
1 cup light brown sugar
2 cups granulated sugar
5 cups all-purpose flour, sifted before measuring
1 teaspoon baking powder
¾ teaspoon salt
2 teaspoons ground nutmeg
1 pound shelled pecans, chopped

Combine the cherries and raisins (or dates) in a bowl. Add the bourbon. Cover with plastic wrap and let soak overnight.

Set the oven to 250 degrees. Grease a tube pan, then line it with baking parchment and grease it again. Or prepare 2 average (9-by-5-inch) or 6 small (6-by3½-inch) bread pans in the same manner. (The smaller ones are perfect for gifts.)

Whip the egg whites until stiff but not dry. Set aside.

Cream the butter and sugars until fluffy. Add the egg yolks and beat well. Add the soaked fruit, including any remaining soaking liquid.

In a separate bowl, combine the sifted flour, baking powder, salt, and nutmeg. Add to the butter mixture. Using a large rubber spatula or wooden spoon, fold in the beaten egg whites. Then add the chopped nuts and stir. The batter will be slightly pink (from the cherries) and quite stiff.

Spoon the dough into the prepared pan (or pans).

If making one large cake, bake 2½ to 3 hours; it is done when top is golden brown and a tester inserted in the center comes out clean.

If making loaf cakes, arrange the pans in the oven so that they don't touch each other. Bake 1½ to 2 hours, or until a tester inserted in the center of each comes out clean. Because ovens tend to hold heat unevenly, it's a good idea to switch the positions of the pans about halfway through the baking time.

Cool briefly. Remove from pans and cool thoroughly. Serve immediately or store by wrapping them in cheesecloth that has been soaked in bourbon. (If making a tube cake, stuff the center hole with bourbon-soaked cheesecloth.) Wrap well in wax paper and keep cool, storing in the refrigerator, if necessary, up to one month.

Yield: 1 large cake, 2 average (9-by-5-inch) loaves, or 6 small (6-by-3½-inch) loaves; at least 12 servings

MOM'S POUND CAKE

Jimmy's mom turns out dozens of these cakes for Christmas presents, and everyone loves to get them. Her recipe makes two large cakes. You can halve it if you like, but why not make two and give one away?

1 pound (4 sticks) unsalted butter
4 cups (1 pound) sugar
12 eggs
4 cups all-purpose flour
1 teaspoon baking powder
½ teaspoon salt
1 teaspoon vanilla extract

Carolyn Kennedy Bowen and Jimmy.

Center a rack in the oven and set the oven to 325 degrees. Grease two 9- or 10-inch tube pans well and set them aside.

In a large bowl, cream the butter thoroughly—an electric mixer is very helpful. Gradually add the sugar and mix until light and fluffy. Add 2 eggs and beat well.

In a small bowl, mix the flour, baking powder, and salt. Add this mixture in batches to the butter mixture, alternating with the remaining 10 eggs, 2 or 3 at a time. Finally, add the vanilla and mix to combine.

Pour the batter into the prepared pans and bake 50 to 60 minutes, or until a tester inserted into the cake comes out clean.

Yield: 2 large cakes, at least 12 servings each

Nicole Graves.

NICOLE'S BOWL CAKE

This "recipe" came about one day when Nicole was taking a perfectly done Sour Cream Chocolate Chip Cake out of the pan and it broke into pieces. Short on time—and not wanting to waste the cake—Nicole made a custard and layered it with the broken-up cake. She topped the whole thing with whipped cream and chocolate shavings, and another River Run favorite was born.

Note: You can make the cake alone; it's a very good dessert on its own. Likewise, you could use this "bowl cake" method to save almost any cake that falls apart.

For the cake:
8 tablespoons (1 stick)
   unsalted butter, melted
1¼ cups sugar
2 eggs
1 cup sour cream
1 tablespoon vanilla extract
2 tablespoons milk
2 cups all-purpose flour
2 teaspoons baking powder
1 teaspoon baking soda
¼ teaspoon salt
6 ounces (1 cup) semisweet
   chocolate chips

For the custard:
1 quart light cream or half-
   and-half
¼ cup all-purpose flour
Generous pinch salt
1 cup sugar
8 egg yolks, well beaten
4 tablespoons (½ stick)
   unsalted butter
4 teaspoons vanilla extract

For serving:
1 pint heavy cream, whipped and flavored with sugar and vanilla
   extract, to taste
Chocolate shavings (optional)

Set the oven to 350 degrees. Grease a 9- or 10-inch tube pan.

Make the cake: In a large bowl, cream together the butter and sugar until fluffy (an electric mixer is useful). Add the eggs, sour cream, vanilla extract and milk, one at a time, beating to mix. Add one cup of the flour and the baking powder, baking soda and salt, and mix well. Add the remining cup of flour and continue to stir or beat until batter looks smooth. Stir in the chocolate chips by hand.

Pour into the prepared pan and bake about 45 minutes, or until a tester inserted in the cake comes out clean.

Remove from the oven and allow to cool for a bit. Remove from the pan and cool further on a rack.

Make the custard: In a saucepan, bring the light cream (or half-and-half) almost to a boil.

In a separate bowl, mix the flour, salt, and sugar. Add to the cream, stirring constantly, until the mixture coats the back of a spoon and reaches 160 degrees on an instant read. Pour some of the hot cream mixture into the egg yolks, then stir the egg yolks into the cream mixture. Keep cooking, stirring all the while, until the mixture thickens and reaches a temperature of 160 degrees on instant-read thermometer. Remove from the heat and add the butter and vanilla, stirring until the butter melts.

To assemble, cut the cake into bite-sized pieces. In a trifle bowl or other serving bowl, layer the cake with the custard. Chill, covered, for several hours or overnight—the dessert should be chilled through. Right before serving, whip the cream, flavor it to taste, and "frost" the dessert. Top with chocolate shavings, if desired.

Yield: at least 10 servings

PLANTATION FUDGE CAKE

This is the cake to make when only a chocolate cake with chocolate frosting will do.

For the cake:
8 tablespoons (1 stick) unsalted butter
4 ounces semisweet chocolate
2 cups granulated sugar
3 eggs
1½ teaspoons vanilla extract
1¼ cups buttermilk
2¼ cups all-purpose flour
1½ teaspoons baking soda
¾ teaspoon salt

For the frosting:
8 tablespoons (1 stick) unsalted butter, at room temperature
1 pound (about 4 cups) confectioner's sugar
2 ounces unsweetened chocolate, melted and cooled
¼ teaspoon salt
1 teaspoon vanilla extract
½ cup heavy cream
½ cup chopped toasted pecans (see note)
Shredded sweetened coconut and/or chocolate shavings, for topping (optional)

Center a rack in the oven and set the oven to 350 degrees. Grease and flour two 9-inch round cake pans and set them aside.

Make the cake: In a large, heavy-bottomed pot or Dutch oven, melt the butter and chocolate together. Remove from the heat. Stir in the sugar, eggs, and vanilla, mixing to combine. Add the buttermilk. Stir in about ½ cup of the flour, then add the baking soda and salt and mix well. Add the remaining flour and mix until the batter is uniform in color and smooth.

Pour the batter into the prepared cake pans and bake 30 to 35 minutes, or until a tester inserted in the center comes out clean. Place the pans on cake racks to cool for a few minutes, then remove the cakes from the pans and allow them to cool completely on the racks.

Meanwhile, make the frosting: Using an electric mixer, cream together all the frosting ingredients except the nuts and coconut. Stir the nuts in by hand.

When the cake layers are thoroughly cooled, frost them evenly. Serve as is, or sprinkle coconut or chocolate shavings or both on top of the cake.

Note: To toast the pecans, put them in an ovenproof skillet in the preheated oven for about 10 minutes. Watch them carefully; nuts burn quickly.

Yield: one 9-inch 2-layer cake, or 8 to 10 servings

Jan Monteagudo Meese.

212

CHOCOLATE MOUSSE PIE

A new and welcome Thanksgiving tradition at our house.

For the crust:
2 generous cups crushed chocolate wafers, about 44 wafers (see note)
¾ cup (1½ sticks) unsalted butter, melted

For filling:
1 pound semisweet chocolate
6 eggs
2 cups heavy cream

For decoration (optional):
Chocolate curls or shavings

Lightly butter the bottom and sides of a 9-inch springform pan.

Make the crust: combine the wafer crumbs and melted butter. Press into the bottom and up the sides of the prepared pan. The crust will go up the sides of the pan about 1½ to 2 inches.

Make the filling: Melt the chocolate in the top of a double boiler over very hot water. Remove from the heat when the chocolate is just melted and can be stirred smooth. Allow to cool a bit—it should read 100 degrees on an instant-read thermometer.

Separate 4 of the eggs, putting the yolks in a small bowl and the whites in a large one. Beat the whites until they are stiff but not dry. Add the 2 remaining whole eggs to the 4 yolks and mix well with a fork.

In another large bowl, beat the heavy cream until stiff peaks form.

Add a large spoonful of the melted chocolate into the bowl with the yolks and stir quickly to combine. Then add this mixture (chocolate and eggs) to the melted chocolate. Scrape the sides of the egg bowl with a rubber spatula to scrape up all of the mixture.

Add about one-third of the whipped cream and one-third of the egg whites to the chocolate mixture and stir well. Then, using a rubber spatula, carefully fold in the remaining whipped cream and egg whites. Mix gently but well; the mixture should turn a uniform brown.

Pour the mousse into the crust, cover with plastic wrap, and refrigerate until thoroughly chilled, at least 6 hours. When ready to serve, carefully remove the sides from the springform pan (you may need to run a table knife around the edges to loosen the crust a bit).

Decorate the top, if desired, with chocolate curls or shavings.

Note: We use Nabisco Famous Wafers for this crust. One package (9 ounces) has about 44 wafers; you can use them all. Crush them in a food processor or put them in a plastic bag and crush them with a rolling pin.

Yield: 10 to 12 servings

CREAM PUFFS

Nicole brought some of these to her first interview for a baking job at River Run: we hired her on the spot. In winter, make the chocolate filling, but when berries are in season, the "summer filling" is a must.

For the cream puff pastry:
1 cup water
8 tablespoons (1 stick) unsalted butter
1 cup all-purpose flour
Generous pinch salt
4 eggs, at room temperature

For the chocolate filling:
8 ounces semisweet chocolate
6 ounces cream cheese (about ¾ cup), at
   room temperature
½ cup confectioner's sugar
¾ cup heavy cream

For the summer filling:
2 cups heavy cream
2 tablespoons confectioner's sugar
1 cup fresh berries, hulled and chopped (if
   necessary), or more to taste

Set the oven to 400 degrees.

**Jay Southgate, steeplejack;
Kim Pierce, physician's assistant, with
Morgan and Bailey Southgate.**

215

Make the pastry: In a saucepan, combine the water and butter and bring to a boil over low heat. Slowly add the flour and salt, stirring constantly until the mixture begins to clear the sides of the pan. Remove from the heat and add the eggs, one at a time, beating quickly and continuously so they don't scramble.

Form this sticky batter into 8 rounded mounds on an ungreased baking sheet. (Each puff will take a generous 2 tablespoons dough.) Place them in a circle, barely allowing them to touch. Bake for 35 to 40 minutes. Allow them to cool, then separate them into individual puffs.

Make the chocolate filling: Chop 6 ounces of the chocolate and melt it in the top of a double boiler over very hot water. Allow it to cool a bit—it should register about 100 degrees on an instant-read thermometer.

In a large mixing bowl, beat the cream cheese and sugar together until very creamy. Beat in the melted chocolate. (No need to wash the double boiler top; you'll be using it again to melt the rest of the chocolate for the topping.)

In another bowl, whip the cream until stiff peaks form. Carefully fold the whipped cream into the chocolate mixture.

Slice the pastry puffs in half horizontally and heap with filling. Put the tops on and place them on a serving platter.

Chop the remaining 2 ounces of chocolate and melt in the top of a double boiler set over very hot water. Drizzle it over the tops of the cream puffs. If some gets on the platter, just consider it "artistic."

Set the cream puffs in a cool place until ready to serve. A little sitting is OK, but don't let them sit for more than an hour or so, or they will get too soggy.

Alternatively, make the summer filling: Beat the heavy cream and sugar until stiff peaks form. Add the fruit and stir to distribute evenly.

Fill the cooled pastry puffs right before serving (the berry filling will make them very soggy even if you fill them a little while before you serve them).

Yield: 8 cream puffs

BILL THE BARBER

As Remembered by His Daughter

His name was William Carroll, but everyone knew him as "Bill the Barber." He, in turn, knew everyone by name. He charged only $1.00 per cut until his customers got him to raise the price to $1.25. However, all his customers got more than just a shave and haircut—there might be a game of checkers or just a chair in which to sit—and if you ever wanted to know what was going on, his shop was *the* place to go. Over his fifty years of barbering, he worked out of several locations, including the basement of the Plainfield Inn (now a used furniture shop) and in the building that now houses River Run.

He was so proud when, at school graduations, he could see his handiwork march down the aisle under the mortarboards of the entire male portion of the class.

He would encourage parents to hold their little ones for that all-important First Haircut. They would take pictures and get him to sign their baby books. He'd visit the sick at home or in the hospital on his time off and even went to the mortuaries to prepare bodies for funerals. He was squeamish about that at first, but he said afterward that his funeral home customers "sure didn't give me any trouble."

Known for his honesty, he was very involved in church leadership as trustee, head usher, and finance chairman for decades. During his tenure the church was never in debt.

He had an apartment behind the barbershop. One day a Methodist pastor chastised him for renting to a single black man with a live-in girlfriend. Bill

217

just set his jaw—"Everyone needs a home and it isn't up to me to judge," he said—and kept right on shaving.

Born in Canada in 1901, he moved with his family to Woodbury, Vermont, at age 11. Loyal to his parents, he helped on the family farm until he was 26 but then moved to Montpelier to learn his trade. He started his fledgling business in Plainfield during the Depression and soon noticed a slim young postal worker (the post office was in the building that was to become his own shop and, eventually, River Run). Dorothy Collins became his bride in October 1933.

He suffered from Parkinson's for nine years before retiring, yet his hand was steady when shaving or cutting hair. He said he would stop when he could no longer turn the key in the lock. One day it happened; he sold the barbershop the next day. In 1984, a day short of his fifty-first wedding anniversary, Bill passed on.

"Well done, thou good and faithful servant."

Ruth M. Carroll Parmenter
January 17, 2000

BROWNIES

The great thing about these brownies, aside from how good they taste, is that you dirty only one pot when making them.

8 tablespoons (1 stick) unsalted butter
12 ounces bittersweet chocolate, chopped
1½ cups sugar
1¼ cups all-purpose flour
2 teaspoons vanilla extract
½ teaspoon baking powder
¼ teaspoon salt
3 eggs

Set oven to 350 degrees. Grease a 13-by-9-inch pan.

In a large, heavy-bottomed saucepan set over low heat, melt the butter and half the chocolate, stirring constantly, until just melted. Stir in the sugar, flour, vanilla, baking powder, salt, and eggs. Stir in the remaining chocolate chunks. Spread in the prepared pan.

Calvin Ulysses Levin Schneider.

Bake 30 minutes, or until a tester comes out just clean. Don't overbake, or the brownies will be tough. Allow to cool completely before cutting.

Yield: a dozen 3-inch-square brownies

BUTTERSCOTCH BROWNIES

These go especially well with a cup of hot unsweetened tea.

    8 tablespoons (1 stick) unsalted butter, at room temperature
    2 cups firmly packed dark brown sugar
    2 eggs
    2 teaspoons vanilla extract
    2½ cups all-purpose flour
    2 teaspoons baking powder
    ½ teaspoon salt
    1 cup chopped pecans or walnuts

Center a rack in the oven and set the oven to 350 degrees. Line a 13-by-9-inch baking pan with aluminum foil and grease the foil.

In a large bowl, cream together the butter and sugar with an electric mixer set on medium speed. Add the eggs and vanilla and beat well. Add about ½ cup of the flour, the baking powder, and salt and continue mixing. Add the rest of the flour. The batter will be extremely stiff. Stir in the nuts with a spoon or knead them in with your hands.

Spread the dough in the prepared pan, smoothing the top with a flat table knife or spatula to make it even.

Bake 20 to 25 minutes, or until a tester inserted in the center comes out clean. Do not overbake, or your brownies will be tough.

Remove from the oven and immediately take the brownies—foil and all—out of the pan. Invert them on a rack so the foil is on top, then peel off the foil. Allow to cool thoroughly before cutting.

Yield: a dozen 3-inch-square brownies

Michael J. Hardy.

EXTREME BROWNIE COOKIES

These are like brownies—chewy and chocolaty—but in cookie shape.

12 ounces (2 cups) bittersweet chocolate, chopped
8 tablespoons (1 stick) unsalted butter
3 eggs
1½ teaspoons vanilla extract
1 cup sugar
½ cup all-purpose flour
1½ teaspoons baking powder
¼ teaspoon salt
6 ounces (1 cup) semisweet chocolate chips
1 cup chopped pecans or walnuts (or a combination)

In the top of a double boiler set over very hot water, melt the bittersweet chocolate and butter. Allow it to cool.

Using an electric mixer, beat the eggs and vanilla in a mixing bowl until frothy. Slowly add the sugar and beat until the mixture ribbons off the beaters. Add the melted chocolate mixture. Stir to combine.

Sift the dry ingredients together. Add to the chocolate mixture and stir to combine. Fold in the chips and nuts. The dough will seem more like cake batter than cookie dough. Cover the mixing bowl with plastic wrap and refrigerate until the dough is well chilled (and more cookie-dough-like).

Set the oven to 350 degrees. Line several baking sheets with baking parchment.

Scoop up the chilled dough and roll with your hands into small balls the size of a whole walnut (in the shell). Place the cookies on the prepared pans, about 1½ inches apart.

Bake about 12 minutes or a bit longer. The tops of the cookies should look dry and cracked. Allow to cool for a minute on the baking sheet, then remove to cake racks for further cooling.

Yield: 4 to 5 dozen cookies

Louie Ducharme.

PEANUT BUTTER CHOCOLATE CHUNK COOKIES

Marialisa's husband, Dirk, says these are the best cookies he has ever tasted. Who are we to disagree?

12 tablespoons (1½ sticks) unsalted butter, at room temperature
½ cup smooth peanut butter (see note #1)
1 cup granulated sugar
1 cup firmly packed light brown sugar
2 eggs
1½ teaspoons vanilla extract
2¼ cups all-purpose flour
1 teaspoon baking soda
Generous pinch salt
12 ounces (2 cups) chopped chocolate: semisweet or a combination of
  semisweet and white chocolate (see note #2)

Set the oven to 375 degrees.

In a large mixing bowl, using an electric mixer set on medium speed, beat together the butter, peanut butter, granulated sugar, brown sugar, eggs, and vanilla.

Add about ½ cup of the flour, the baking soda, and salt and mix thoroughly. Add the remaining flour and mix well. By hand, stir in the chocolate.

Ben Cohen, Aretha, and Waggles.

Scoop out the dough with a ¼-cup measure, and drop onto an ungreased cookie sheet, spacing the globs of dough about 2½ inches apart. Bake for 11 to 12 minutes, until just turning golden. Allow the cookies to cool for a couple of minutes on the pan, then remove them carefully to a rack (they are fragile when hot) and allow them to cool completely.

Note #1: Brand-name peanut butter works well here. If you use "natural" peanut butter made without salt, you may want to increase the salt by at least ¼ teaspoon.

Note #2: We use twelve 1-ounce squares of Baker's chocolate (6 ounces semisweet, 6 ounces white), and cut each square into 6 pieces. Large chocolate morsels, available in the baking section of grocery stores, would also work, but we like the effect of the irregular chunks from chopping it ourselves.

Yield: eighteen 3- to 4-inch cookies

AUNT HAZEL'S FRIED FRUIT PIES

Hazel Schissler.

Aunt Hazel lived right across the yard from Jimmy when he was growing up. He has fond memories of walking home across that yard on many occasions with a fried peach or apple pie cooling in a paper towel.

½ pound dried apples or peaches
Sugar, to taste
1 recipe biscuit dough (page 64)
Oil, for frying (about 1½ cups for a 10-inch skillet)

Cook the dried fruit, covered in water, at a low boil until nice and tender, 20 to 30 minutes. Drain and mash as you would mash potatoes. Add sugar to the sweetness you like and let cool.

Meanwhile, make the biscuit dough but knead it a little more so you can handle it better. Roll the dough on a floured board to about ⅛ inch thick. Place a saucer, 6½ or 7 inches across, on top of the dough and cut around it with a sharp knife. Repeat until you have 10 rounds.

Place 2 to 3 tablespoons of fruit on one half of each round of dough and fold the other side over it. Mash the edges together with a fork to seal them. Stick each pie with a fork 3 or 4 times to make steam holes in the top.

In a heavy skillet, heat about ½ inch of oil until very hot—the surface should look wavy. Fry the pies, 2 at a time, flipping over when each side is nice and brown, 3 to 5 minutes per side. Drain on paper towels and serve immediately.

Yield: about a 10 pies, or 10 servings

PORCH LEMONADE

Dust off the porch rocker, plunk a pitcher of this by your side, and you're set for summer. Be forewarned: this lemonade disappears quickly—you may want to double the recipe.

¾ cup sugar

4½ cups water

Zest of 1 lemon, cut into thin strips

2 cups freshly squeezed lemon juice

2 to 3 tablespoons grenadine, to taste

Mint leaves and/or lemon slices, for garnish (optional)

Porch of River Run.

In a small saucepan, combine the sugar, ½ cup of the water, and lemon zest and bring to a boil, stirring frequently. Reduce the heat and simmer for about 5 minutes, stirring occasionally. Remove from the heat and allow to cool. Strain, discarding the zest. Cover and chill the syrup thoroughly. Chill the remaining 4 cups water.

When the sugar syrup and remaining quart of water are chilled, mix them together, adding the lemon juice and the grenadine. Pour over crushed ice and garnish with mint and sliced lemon, if desired.

Yield: about 1½ quarts, or six 8-ounce servings

MULLED WINE

We don't sell wine, beer, or liquor at River Run (when we're open for dinner, it's B.Y.O.), but we make this warm drink at home during the winter holidays.

> ¾ cup sugar
> ½ cup water
> ½ teaspoon whole cloves
> 2 sticks cinnamon
> Two 2-inch pieces lemon peel
> Two 2-inch pieces orange peel
> 1 bottle (750 ml) dry red wine

Mix the sugar, water, spices, and citrus peels in a pot large enough to hold all the ingredients; bring to a boil. Reduce the heat and simmer about 5 minutes, stirring occasionally. Add the wine and heat until very hot but not boiling.

Serve, straining out the spices and citrus peels with a small strainer (a tea strainer works well).

Yield: about a quart, or five 6-ounce servings

RUSSIAN TEA

Jimmy's mom always makes Russian Tea for special occasions and holidays. Why it's called Russian Tea, we do not know. We always drink it hot (sometimes, with rum) as a holiday punch, but Marialisa discovered it makes a great summer drink, served chilled, over ice with a sprig of mint.

3 quarts water
6 tea bags
2½ cups pineapple juice
1½ cups orange juice
6 tablespoons lemon juice
1½ cups sugar

Bring a quart of the water to a boil and steep the tea bags in it to make a strong tea. Discard the tea bags.

In a large pot, mix together the remaining 2 quarts water, the juices and sugar. Mix in the tea.

Heat through before serving, or chill, and serve over ice.

Yield: about gallon, or 20 6-ounce servings

Plainfield United Methodist Church.

Howard Norman, writer, with family: Jane Shore, poet;
Emma, and cat Scott.

AFTERWORD

VILLAGE LIFE by Howard Norman

In May of 1991, thirty Estonian ballerinas touring the U.S. sunbathed topless in Viiu Ni-
iler and Chet Cole's backyard. Chet and Viiu are artists who work in glass. "Chet served
them watermelon," Viiu told me on a Thursday. Later the same morning I related this an-
ecdote to Maya Kennedy, one of the owner/founders of River Run Restaurant, in Plainfield, Vermont. Then I ordered oatmeal with fruit and nuts. Of course, coffee.

My friend Rick Levy is town constable of Plainfield, a village. When I telephone him or he
telephones me, and one of us says, "Breakfast Friday morning?" we don't have to ask
where.

230

"Where's Jimmy?" Jimmy Kennedy is the other owner/founder and husband of Maya. And the chef. "Fishing tournament," Maya says. Everyone within earshot nods, understanding the emotional dimensions of such events to Jimmy.

After a long search I found a copy of *Letters from Holland,* by the Czech fabulist Karel Cäpek, at Ben Koenig's Country Bookshop, just down the street from River Run. Some mornings my entire axis is River Run/Country Bookshop; if it's raining it rounds out a perfect morning. Undisturbed at the counter, I read *Letters from Holland* straight through; three cups of coffee. *Letters from Holland,* it turns out, was written mostly in Edinburgh.

Here is a letter written by River Run aficionado David Mamet: 5: May: 96 —*

> Dear Howard:
>
> WE MISS YOU AND JANE AND EMMA
> When are you all coming back?
> Thank you for the lovely books.
> We are well, thank God, and completely enervated by Cabin Fever.
> It snowed one million feet this winter, and it is just BARELY on the verge of Spring,
>   and Becca is insane with longing for Flowers.
> I'm working away as usual . . .
> Maya's is Chinese in the Evenings, very nice. Though we do miss our Thurs Nite pork
>   chops.
> Bill and Trish don't open for another 10 days . . .
> nightmare.
> COME BACK.
>
> Love,
>   DM

One Saturday morning Jane, Emma, and I drove from East Calais to Plainfield to eat breakfast at River Run. We sat at the big middle table. Elegant Nessa Rabin said, "Cof-

---

*I hope that David doesn't mind me sharing this letter, which, like his friendship, I cherish. It strikes me as a most intimate composition, perfect equation between WINTER and DESIRE and LOCAL FLAVOR and LOCAL KNOWLEDGE. (Bill and Trish are the dear owners and chefs of Rainbow Sweets Café, out on Route 2 in Marshfield; their establishment is a tradition commensurately irreplaceable in all of our hearts.) For a year or so, genius chef Steve Bogart cooked Chinese food at River Run. Jane, Emma, and I made a "lifetime reservation." It is difficult, really, to explain just how early on a bitter February morning in Vermont one began thinking about Chinese soup.

fee?" The blackboard menus are the size of Arrival/Departure boards in certain one-room rural train depots in Canada I've waited hours in. Charlotte Potok, potter, mother of Maya, came in, sat down, had a quick bite, stood by the cash register schmoozing, then left. Bob and Leda came in. Gus came in. Helen and Jules came in. David and Rebecca and Clara came in. Noah Mamet wasn't born yet. Everybody had a big breakfast. It was snowing. I walked over to the Country Bookshop and found a long-sought-after copy of *An Emotional Memoir of Franz Kline,* by Fielding Dawson. I walked back to River Run. Rick and Rhea didn't come in; we were disappointed. Jane, Emma, and I had the oatmeal, with a side of bacon, juice, coffee. Emma was nine. "What's with Jimmy and catfish, anyway?" Emma said, noting prodigious catfish paraphernalia, totems, and a 1700s print of a catfish by Mark Catesby, let alone the significant number of dishes that include catfish on the menu. "I guess maybe he grew up with them, huh?" (It turned out that Rick and Rhea were in NYC.)

One evening—just at dusk—I was driving home from looking at kingfishers and passed by River Run. Slowing down the car, I looked through the window. I saw a bunch of friends having dinner. I don't know why I didn't go in. I just didn't. I was happy at the sight all the same. That night I had a dream right out of a poem by Blas De Otero or Carlos Drummond De Andrade, in which, insomniacs that they were, they sat up all night thinking without envy of their friends sleeping peacefully, each in their own beds. The world in perfect order. In fact, it was a rare night of solid sleep for me. I dreamt of Uli and Michael in their bed, Rick and Rhea, David and Becky, Ed and Curtis, Roy and Gabrielle, Rick and Andrea, Andrew and Nadelle, Michael and Linda, all peacefully asleep in their beds, a full moon flooding the fields with light. Charlotte and Scott, David and Jody, Alexandra in her bed surrounded by books, Bill and Trish deeply asleep, Joyce asleep with the radio on, and I woke up immediately, thinking it was just like a poem by Blas De Otero. Chet and Viiu, safe in their bed. Larry and Susannah under the moon in Boston. No worries at all, none of us. Barry and Lorrie in their bed by the lake. Ellen and Fran asleep, their big dogs on the moonlit lawn.

Between Ennui and Ecstasy unwinds our whole experience of Time.

When I lived in Greenland, the Inuit villagers who took me in had a phrase—a kind of verbal shrug of resignation and untold experience—that accommodated the most eccentric, vile, untoward, generous, suspect, redundant, unforeseen, self-serving, animated, ill-fated, or redemptive of behaviors, the full human gamut. They would say, "It's village life."

232

Four young men, Goddard College students, long hair under knit hats, wearing greatcoat-length winter coats, traipse into River Run, sit at a corner table. They look somewhat shell-shocked, sullen, silent. Where have I seen their postures and staring-into-the-middle-distance demeanors? Then it occurs to me; they remind me of young men just returned home in Ken Burns's Civil War documentary, as if they'd walked right out of a daguerreotype.

The couple had visited Dublin. Back home in Vermont, cooling night air on T-shirt and blouse. They walked home to their farmhouse built in 1841, having eaten strawberries and whipped cream at a neighbor's. Their daughter away at a "sleepover." On the dirt road, not a word passed between them. Fox bark on the moonlit hill. They stepped into their kitchen. The wife said, "You—*we*—forgot to leave a light on. We must've known." They made love on the sofa, thick pillows tossed aside. The delay caused by suggesting the upstairs bedroom would have been "time flashing to anguish." In any marriage, I'm pretty sure, there are overlapping successions of sleep. She fell asleep; he did not. When she awoke, he was at the kitchen table. "Are you all right?" she said. "I'm reading Bassani again," he said. "*The Smell of Hay*. From that London bookstore. Do you want to sleep upstairs? It's cooler down here, though." She rubbed her face as if washing it with air. "Upstairs," she said. "But with the fans going."

Charlotte, Jimmy, Josie, and Maya, safe in their beds on East Hill.

Ragged ghosts of Civil War soldiers—the oldest, age twenty—sit along the stone wall, across from River Run, on the average summer evening. The AA meeting lets out of the church.

In the morning Tom Slayton offered a lovely, elegiac, unflinching portrait of Vermont poet Hayden Carruth on Vermont Public Radio. I savored it, made a note to order a copy. However, it was followed by a succession of the worst sort of sanctimonious VPR "commentators" dumbing-down on purpose (condescending, that is) in order to please some convenient notion of the "general listener." I drove to River Run. It was my only possible antidote. I had the oatmeal with fruit and nuts, coffee; then I walked over to the Country Bookshop.

My VPR weather report—a fantasy. "Thank goodness the clouds keep us unconsoled."

I simply don't mind anymore that the splendid baker/anthropologist Jules Rabin (who bakes River Run bread with his splendid painter and baker wife/partner, Helen) inadvertently called me a "summer person." It's not necessarily the vocabulary of exclusion; it's simply village life. Note how far the Inuit have helped me come in my thinking? "Snowbird." "Flatlander." "Summer person." Cumulatively, on and off, and at first in quite separate lives, Jane and I have lived in Vermont for about seventy years.

Someone once referred to Rabin bread as "historical." Nessa asleep in her bed. Jules and Helen asleep in their bed, deer surveying their garden. Down their long, wooded road, Dan and Betsy asleep in their bed.

Since he could not sleep, he toured his farmhouse. There was little new in this. It better should have been tea, but he percolated some coffee, drank a cup, an accompaniment to being awake, not the cause. This night would be less wretched because he had learned to consider insomnia a kind of expertise. The farmhouse was built in 1841. He got up from bed; out the second-floor window there was a startlingly moonlit field. The crab apple tree could be seen almost in its entirety. His wife was asleep. His daughter was asleep, her window looking out on the barn. That morning his wife had completed a poem about the man who built their house, Will Peck. It was a balmy summer night at 3 A.M. He had never kept a *Journal of Insomnia*. In this situation, his friend DM would have had tea. He felt like meeting DM in the Village Restaurant in Hardwick or, best scenario, in River Run. But it was 3 A.M.; no restaurant was open. He could not by all etiquette telephone, though DM would have embraced the reason. Crickets were thrumming in the mudroom. Its broken ceiling, mouse entries, torn screen door made it "open to the elements." Both an interior and exterior space. When it comes to coffee, "percolated," he thought, wasn't a word much used these days. In the downstairs rooms it occurred to him that on most every wall was a bird print. In this regard the house was like an historical aviary. These prints were the result of the only form of acquisitiveness he was not ashamed about, except for the beloved house itself. It was in 1973 that he had purchased his first bird art, *Bengal Crow*, 1785, by Aart Schouman (1710–1792), at auction for $2,400. That comprised one-fifth of his income that year. In 1979 he sold it for $8,500 to the exact same person who had auctioned it off in 1973, who had written to him, "I've from day one thought it was a mistake to let it go." He used the money to pay rent on an apartment in Toronto, to travel and work in the Arctic, and to send a down payment on *Parrot*, by Edward Lear, to a private owner living in San Francisco. Once you put your name out there, notices of bird art come in fairly often. In a catalogue from a famous auction house he saw, in 1984, *Bengal Crow*; later he learned

234

it had sold for $13,000. He wondered if some ill fate had befallen the seller (or if in a few years the seller would write the new owner a letter).

Julie and Ella safely asleep in their beds, in their house by the lake in New Hampshire.

One night, very very late, lying awake in the guest room so as not to disturb his wife, reading *The Cryptogram*, he heard a car go past, "Duke of Earl" on its radio. It brought back some memories. Memories from even before the song was recorded. Like of his older brother's girlfriend, whose name was Paris. That was in 1959. Paris often wore a tight-fitting T-shirt that said EXIST TO KISS YOU. (His introduction to existentialism.) She kept a pet cockatoo. His brother had fixed a hook to the back seat's ceiling of his 1948 Buick so that Paris could hang up the cockatoo's cage while they were driving around. The Buick, a black hippopotamus of a car, had the word TURBOGLIDE in beautiful silver cursive letters flowing across the dashboard. Gray plush interior. Eight ashtrays. He was having a lot of trouble learning to write cursive in elementary school. Paris suggested that he take a pen and paper, sit in the front seat, and using the word TURBOGLIDE as a model, practice his handwriting. (He was nervous about the "cursive example" due in a week.) So whenever the car was in the driveway, he practiced. Mainly he wrote the word TURBOGLIDE. Sometimes he constructed complete sentences chronicling present-tense incidents, e.g., "He sat in the TURBOGLIDE while Paris and his brother made out in the back seat." He got an A- on his next cursive example, an improvement of two grades.

Will Hamlin safe in his bed on Maple Hill, who embodies the philosophical dignity of the village.

Q. Mr. Borges, may I ask you a philosophical question?

Jorge Luis Borges: As you wish.

Q. What is your idea of heaven?

Jorge Luis Borges: A restaurant where a blind man such as I wants to memorize the menu like a poem, and when I leave, I want to shake hands with the waiters.

Jody and Brad (when they visited Vermont, they had three meals in a row at River Run) asleep in their bed in Maryland.

Whenever I walk past the waterfall across the street from River Run, I think of Osip Mandelstam's phrase: "New-fallen singing water."

I phone Rick Levy and we talk about ironing. It turns out he and I have different strategies. He irons the sleeves of a shirt first, followed by the shoulders and back, ending with the collar, "to avoid obvious collar wrinkle," as he puts it. For some reason I do the collar first. I conjecture that it might be a technique born of being in a hurry and ironing only the collar, since that is all that shows at the top of a sweater. "What about in summer?" he says. I have no answer.

Stepping out of the Country Bookshop one morning, I look over to River Run. Gauzy pale moon still in the sky. Down the steep grade from Route 2, Rick, in leather jacket, on his motorcycle. He parks out front of the restaurant. He stretches as if yawning, then lifts the helmet off his head. Constable Levy looks to be savoring the moment, the *anticipation* ("The infinite passion of expectation," as Gina Berriault wrote) of maybe a cup of coffee, oatmeal, home fries, perhaps an *omelet*. "And a side of—." He does not need to be interrupted, I thought, before a day's work in the Prisoner's Rights Office in Montpelier. Though truth be told, he is the one person I most need to speak with. I have a beautiful photograph taken by Rick Levy in Spain.

Photographs of neighbors taken all over the world, each wearing a River Run T-shirt or sweatshirt, are posted on the wall next to the counter. In remarkably diverse locales, all over the world.

River Run Hot Sauce makes you, as Uli Belenky said, "Alert."

Bitter cold March night. Irreversible loss of an old dear friendship. Village life. Sit in River Run, waiting for dinner companions. Write a letter to California. Sleet mixed with snow. "What good is intelligence if you can't discover a useful melancholy?" (Ryunosuke Akutagawa)

The food is so good you could weep.

236

ABOUT THE AUTHORS

JIMMY KENNEDY (*recipes*) was born and raised in Brewer, Mississippi, where he learned to cook from his mother, Carolyn Kennedy Bowen. He holds a degree in Business from Ole Miss, and his career includes a stint selling Mississippi catfish to New York City restaurants. When not cooking at River Run, Jimmy is either at home with Maya and their baby daughter, Josie, or bass fishing on Lake Champlain.

MAYA KENNEDY (*graphics*) was born in the U.S. Virgin Islands and raised in Plainfield, Vermont. She is a graphic artist and designer, and illustrated *The Duck and The Goat*, a children's book written by David Mamet. She also works the front of the house at River Run.

MARIALISA CALTA (*text*) is a Vermont-based freelance writer whose work has appeared in many national publications, including the *New York Times, Gourmet* and *Food & Wine*. Her weekly column, "Food," is syndicated by United Media. She lives with her husband and daughters in Calais, Vermont, about 12 miles too far from River Run.

INDEX

239

240

241

OLD COLORADO CITY

LE PONT
DE LA CHUTE

RIVER RUN

I'm good eatin!

SMALL CAN, BIG FOOD

A LITTLE SOUL FOOD UP NORTH

FINE AS FROG HAIR

ROAD
SHOW

DOC GRANT'S
Restaurant & Gift Shop
Halfway Between the Equator
and the North Pole

EQUATOR
3107 miles

NORTH POLE
3107 miles

ALTITUDE 1547 FEET
RANGELEY, MAINE

RIVER RUN